THE
HUDSON-FULTON
CELEBRATION

**Celebration medal, honoring Henry
Hudson on one side and Robert Fulton
on the other**

THE
HUDSON-FULTON
CELEBRATION

New York's River Festival of 1909 and the Making of a Metropolis

Kathleen Eagen Johnson

☞ Historic Hudson Valley

Fordham University Press · New York · 2009

Support has been provided by the *We the People* initiative of the
National Endowment for the Humanities. Any views, findings, conclusions, or recommendations expressed in this publication do
not necessarily reflect those of the National Endowment for the
Humanities.

Additional support has been provided by Emigrant Bank and
the Milstein Family, and by Furthermore, a program of the J. M.
Kaplan Fund.

Fordham University Press has no responsibility for the persistence
or accuracy of URLs for external or third-party Internet websites
referred to in this publication and does not guarantee that any content on such websites is, or will remain, accurate or appropriate.

Library of Congress Cataloging-in-Publication Data

Johnson, Kathleen Eagen.
  The Hudson-Fulton Celebration : New York's river festival of 1909
and the making of a metropolis / Kathleen Eagen Johnson.—1st ed.
      p. cm.
  Includes bibliographical references and index.
  ISBN 978-0-8232-3021-1 (cloth : alk. paper)
1. Hudson-Fulton Celebration, 1909. 2. Hudson, Henry, d. 1611—
Anniversaries, etc. 3. Fulton, Robert, 1765–1815—Anniversaries, etc.
4. Hudson River (N.Y. and N.J.)—Anniversaries, etc. 5. New York (N.Y.)—
Anniversaries, etc. 6. New York (N.Y.)—History—1898–1951. 7. Festivals—New York (State)—New York—History—20th century. I. Title.
  F127.H8J66 2009
  974.7'1041—dc22   2008050168

11 10 09   5 4 3 2 1
First edition
Printed in China

Above: Replica *Clermont* before New York skyline, September 25, 1909

Contents

HUDSON~FULTON
CELEBRATION

HUDSON ★ WRIGHT ★ PEARY
FULTON ★ CURTIS ★ COOK

NEW YORK CITY
SEPT 25th~OCT. 9th 1909
COPYRIGHT

A Special Message

It is my pleasure to write a special message for *The Hudson-Fulton Celebration: New York's River Festival of 1909 and the Making of a Metropolis.* This important book offers a window into life in New York City and the Hudson River Valley during the exciting time immediately before World War I. The Hudson-Fulton Celebration—a cross between a world's fair, a historical pageant, and a land and water carnival—was designed to honor Henry Hudson and Robert Fulton, two men whose exploits on the Hudson River had gained them entry into American history's hall of fame. In the autumn of 1909, millions of New Yorkers and their out-of-town guests gathered in cities and towns along the Hudson River to honor the achievements of these men. As Kate Johnson convincingly argues, the event was actually more expressive of the issues preoccupying New Yorkers in 1909 than of the historical figures and events it was designed to commemorate. Through this appealing volume, Kate invites us to think about the role public history plays in American lives and communities, then and now.

In talking with Kate and reading her manuscript, I was fascinated to learn how members of my own family helped support the Celebration and how it, in turn, touched their lives. My great-grandfather, John D. Rockefeller, contributed $5,000 to the Hudson-Fulton Celebration Fund, making him one of its most generous financial supporters. My grandfather, John D. Rockefeller, Jr., recorded his pleasure in viewing the parades and the nighttime electrical displays. He found the sight of Wilbur Wright flying in his biplane the most thrilling of all. My grandmother, Abby Aldrich Rockefeller, took advantage of the Celebration's art offerings. She toured the Metropolitan Museum, where two pioneering loan exhibitions—one of seventeenth-century Dutch Master paintings and the other featuring early American art and antiques—attracted huge crowds. Earlier in 1909, her father, United States Senator Nelson W. Aldrich, had written a piece of legislation that removed an existing tariff on art and antiquities imported into America. Its passage prompted J. P. Morgan and Benjamin Altman to bring Dutch paintings to New York in time for the Celebration. Happily for my grandmother and thousands of other art lovers, Morgan, Altman, and other early collectors believed that it was a privilege to share their art holdings with the American public. This belief in "art for the people" underscored the Empire State's vibrant tradition of philanthropy in the arts arena and helped make New York City a world capital of arts and culture during the twentieth century.

The founding and strengthening of cultural institutions in New York did not start and stop with the 1909 Hudson-Fulton Celebration. Nearly fifty years later, my grandfather created a historical organization now called Historic Hudson Valley. Drawing on some of the same characters, events, and places organizers spotlighted at that commemorative festival long ago, Historic Hudson Valley continues to explore the topic of New York history through the centuries and to relate it to contemporary events. By mounting a program of public history at six historic sites, on the web, and through publications, the staff of Historic Hudson Valley engages a twenty-first-century audience in a conversation about how the past can inform topics of interest today.

The sensibility that Kate has applied to this project epitomizes the organizational values of Historic Hudson Valley, an institution charged with the dual mission to preserve the region's history and to educate the public about it. She has tackled a complex topic, weaving together a wide range of facts and images into an interesting narrative. She invites readers into the story, encouraging them to appreciate how and why the people of the past held different points of view about the same event. Keeping in mind that learners absorb information in different ways, Kate has supplemented the book with an online exhibition mounted on Historic Hudson Valley's website www.hudsonvalley.org, a curriculum guide for educators and students, and other programs. I thank and congratulate Kate and her colleagues for their work in bringing this event in New York history to light so successfully.

This handsomely illustrated history pays tribute to a city, a river, and a region that mean a great deal to me. I hope that you, too, enjoy *The Hudson-Fulton Celebration: New York's River Festival of 1909 and the Making of a Metropolis.*

Mark F. Rockefeller

Preface

Most people don't realize that New York began as a business venture. Indeed, the development of the city and lower Hudson Valley has had an unparalleled spirit of enterprise for 400 years. People came to improve their own economic situations and, as they did so, their hard work supported the city's dynamic growth and undying entrepreneurial spirit.

Emigrant Savings Bank was founded in 1850 to help fund the life and business needs of the thousands of immigrants who poured into New York each year. In fact, Emigrant's steadfast presence predates many of the city's other great landmarks and institutions. Indeed, Emigrant funded a number of those landmarks. The contract to build St. Patrick's Cathedral was signed at Emigrant headquarters. Emigrant went on to finance the building of many of the great churches of the New York Archdiocese. Emigrant's portfolio of bonds included funding for the public works project that became Central Park. Over the years, Emigrant was a key part of the economic engine that drove the development of the region. Through the selling of War Bonds and War Savings and Thrift Stamps, and innovations such as special passbook jackets for depositors, Emigrant became the largest savings bank in the country by 1925. In 1986, the Bank was acquired by our family and became a private stock bank. Today, Emigrant and its holding company, New York Private Bank & Trust, is the largest privately held bank in the country. Many institutions have come and gone, but Emigrant survives—primarily because it represents the classic New York tradition of struggle, improvement, and success.

Emigrant was also a springboard to the American Dream. Even while working as laborers or domestic servants, many immigrants still managed to save, some accumulating the modern equivalent of $10,000 or more before they had been in New York for even a decade. As Emigrant Savings Bank's depositors evolved into a middle class growing in number and diversity, they and others contributed to the emergence of New York City as a world financial capital.

It was the Hudson-Fulton Celebration of 1909 that marked the city's new status. During this event, New York's diverse population and its strong embrace of capitalism were acknowledged internationally as distinctive, modern, and uniquely American. At the same time, however, Americans were grappling with hard economic times as well as social, technological, and transformational challenges. Emigrant Savings Bank played a key role for both depositors and borrowers in overcoming these challenges—just as it does today. It is appropriate, therefore, that Emigrant supports this volume which captures the tensions as well as the exuberance of New York's tercentenary celebration.

It is equally fitting that the latest step in Emigrant's evolution has resulted in our presence in the Hudson Valley town of Ossining, New York. In 2004, we launched EmigrantDirect, an internet banking service that symbolizes how far the financial services industry has evolved in helping people achieve their dreams since the early days of Emigrant Bank.

No one is better qualified than Historic Hudson Valley's Kate Johnson to undertake this retrospective. She has written extensively about the properties once owned by the Philipses, the Van Cortlandts, the Livingstons, the Rockefellers, and Washington Irving as well as the contributions made by these New Yorkers.

Among Irving's achievements was convincing his friend John Jacob Astor to give his collection of books to serve as the foundation of the New York Public Library. In addition, the Public Library's Irma and Paul Milstein Division of United States History, Local History and Genealogy, named in honor of my parents, is one of the largest collections of New York history. The Public Library also holds many historical documents of Emigrant Savings Bank. These resources are vital to the exhaustive research that makes possible projects like this book.

My own commitment to New York's current and future vibrancy as a hub of economic, civic, and cultural activity and my wife Abby's involvement as a trustee of the New York Public Library make this book significant to me. It is my hope that you too will find this exploration of innovation, entrepreneurship, and the American Dream through the lens of this celebration meaningful.

Howard P. Milstein

Chairman, New York Private Bank & Trust and Emigrant Bank

Acknowledgments

This book has been a long time in the making. I began research-ing the topic of the Hudson-Fulton Celebration in a serious way for a paper "From Frans Hals to Windmills: The Arts and Crafts Fascination with Lowlands Culture," delivered at the Winterthur Museum conference *Substance of Style: New Perspectives on the Arts and Crafts Movement* in 1990. Over the years, with the aid of many generous colleagues, I continued to collect references to New York's fab-ulous history fair. I am delighted to have the opportunity to present this mate-rial through a book and online exhibition mounted on Historic Hudson Valley's website www.hudsonvalley.org. I also want to recognize those who have helped the project come to fruition.

Deepest thanks go to my partner in many museological projects at Historic Hudson Valley, Margaret L. Vetare, who generously applied her amazing intellect and countless hours to shaping, strengthening, and copyediting the text. I am extremely lucky to count her as a colleague and a friend. My equally wonderful co-worker Anne Goslin displayed her massive organizational talent and calm good humor to managing images and rights. Once again I had the extreme pleas-ure of collaborating with graphic designer Steven Schoenfelder, whose refined approach, unerring eye, and supreme attention to detail make book-making a delight. He was aided ably by the skilled Chris Zichello and Nancy Wolff. I also want to thank Bob Oppedisano, Loomis Mayer, and Kathleen O'Brien-Nicholson at Fordham University Press as well as the enthusiastic Lyn DelliQuadri, Jane Lahr, and Ann Tanenbaum of LTD Editions.

Many champions of this region's history currently or formerly associated with Historic Hudson Valley contributed to the project. Chief among them is Waddell W. Stillman, the president of Historic Hudson Valley, who showed con-sistent belief in the importance of this topic and this project. Librarian Catalina Hannan tracked down microfilm, books, and images with her usual good cheer. Modern-day antiquarian Rob Yasinsac scoured museum and library repositories as a resources scout. Melissa McAteer and Susan Greenstein reviewed the text with diligence. Intern Margaret Staudter skillfully organized the bibliography and assisted with image management. Ray Armater, Laurén Bailey, Geoffrey Carter, Ross W. Higgins, Lynda Jones, Michael Lord, Brian McCoy, David Parsons, Peter Pockriss, Rob Schweitzer, Karen M. Sharman, McKelden Smith, Nancy Struve, and Bill Thompson among others helped make the book, online exhibition, and related programs a reality. My smart and hardworking colleagues at Historic Hudson Valley find inspiration in presenting and preserving the history and material culture of this region.

I am, of course, very grateful to the project's funders. The *We the People* initiative of the National Endowment for the Humanities supported aspects of research, development, and scholarly consultation for the book and online exhibition. I also want to express my gratitude to Emigrant Bank and the Milstein Family for their generous support and to thank Howard P. Milstein and Historic Hudson Valley Trustee Mark F. Rockefeller for providing thoughtful and thought-provoking prefaces. A grant from Joan Davidson and Furthermore, a program of the J. M. Kaplan Fund, provided much-appreciated support. The Honorable Maurice Hinchey of the United States House of Representatives helped secure funding for the project as well.

Deepest thanks go to Chairman Michael Hegarty and the other members of Historic Hudson Valley's Board of Trustees who generously support, and care so deeply for, this wonderful organization in an ongoing way: Jan P. Adelson, Patricia D. Altschul, Kent L. Barwick, Karen H. Bechtel, Nancy N. Campbell, Katharine Chapman, Robert G. DeLaMater, Barbara F. Israel, Herbert E. Nass, William F. Plunkett, Jr., Margaret A. Race, Joseph A. Rice, Charles P. Rockefeller, Mark F. Rockefeller, Arthur Samberg, Molly Schaefer, William Kelly Simpson, David Swope, Thomas D. Thacher II, Charles J. Urstadt, Donald C. Waite III, Paul F. Wallace, and William H. Wright II.

I also wish to thank scholars who reviewed the manuscript. The "dean of New York history," Kenneth T. Jackson, Jacques Barzun Professor of History and the Social Sciences and Director of the Herbert H. Lehman Center for American History at Columbia University, gave the manuscript a critical read and contributed a comprehensive and discerning foreword. There is no more qualified scholar to place New York City within the context of urban history. Similarly, Judith Giuriceo-Lord, Curator of Exhibits and Media at the Statue of Liberty and Ellis Island Immigration Museum of the National Park Service, volunteered precious time to review the manuscript. This expert in the history of immigration and acculturation posed many insightful questions and strengthened the text in many ways.

Thanks go to all those who directed me to images, documents, artifacts, and publications. They include: Marie Long at the New York Botanical Garden, Kenneth Rose at the Rockefeller Archive Center, Liselle LaFrance and Mary Doehla at Historic Cherry Hill in Albany, Stacy Pomeroy Draper at the Rensselaer County Historical Society, W. Douglas McCombs and Ruth Greene-McNally at the Albany Institute of History and Art, Bruce Naramore formerly at Clermont State Historic Site, Greta Bahnemann at the Knight Visual Resources Facility at Cornell Library, David Schuyler at Franklin & Marshall College, Roger T. Reed at Illustration House, Margaret Hofer and Jill Slaight at the New-York Historical Society, Charles Sachs and Carey Stumm at the New York Transit Museum, Amelia Peck at the Metropolitan Museum of Art, Robert Boyle at the Field Library of Peekskill, John Curran at the Peekskill Museum, Joyce Finnerty at the Croton-on-Hudson Historical Society, Sarah Mascia at the Historical Society of the Tarrytowns, and Susan Lane at the Yorktown Historical Society. Special thanks go to Ellen Paul Denker and Bert Denker. Bert and Ellen have offered constant encouragement and research leads since Bert organized the *Substance of Style* conference at the Winterthur Museum, Library & Gardens nearly two decades ago. Laura Beach, Veronique Fehmers, Susan Larkin, Sally Naramore, Bill Ochs, Robert Polastre, John Porter, Frank Racette, Janis Sarubbi, and Barbara Weeks also shared ideas and resources. Thank you.

I also want to thank Betty and Paul Eagen, and all the other Eagens, even if their names are Louden, Williams, or Werner. My parents instilled in all of us a deep love of the Hudson River and its history. Last but not least is Greg Johnson, the unsung hero, who made this all possible.

Kathleen Eagen Johnson

Curator, Historic Hudson Valley

Foreword

In 1909, when millions of enthusiastic spectators lined parade routes and river banks to commemorate the tercentenary of Henry Hudson's epic 1609 voyage to the New World, the Empire City and the Empire State were finally emerging onto the national and international stages. By contrast, in the colonial period, New York City had lagged behind both Boston and Philadelphia in patriotism, population, and economic significance, and New York colony was something of a poor cousin to important provinces like Pennsylvania, Massachusetts, and Virginia.

All this changed during the intervening centuries, as the once small community at the southern tip of Manhattan Island swept past Boston by 1790, Philadelphia by 1810, and Mexico City by 1830. At the time of the American Civil War, New York was one of only a handful of urban centers anywhere to exceed one million inhabitants. Then, in 1898, the Bronx, Brooklyn, Queens, and Staten Island came together with Manhattan to form a gigantic municipality of 300 square miles and 3.4 million people. Soon New York would surpass London as the capital of capitalism, the capital of the twentieth century, and the capital of the world.

New York was not just big in population in 1909; it was different from other world cities like London, Paris, Berlin, and Tokyo in a myriad of ways. First, Gotham was ethnically and racially diverse. Unlike the metropolitan centers of Europe and Asia, New York had never really had a majority culture. The Dutch, who had founded New Amsterdam in 1624, wanted to make money, not save souls. Thus, they were more anxious to do business than to debate the finer points of Protestant theology. Seventeenth-century Manhattan was essentially open to all, and so it has remained ever since.

If the United States was a new kind of nation, where citizenship was based on shared ideals rather than shared bloodlines, so New York City became its outward symbol and its most notable point of entry, a place where newcomers from many lands could find the opportunity for a fresh start. In 1909, for example, the Hudson River Metropolis had more Irish than Dublin, more Italians than Naples, and more Germans than Hamburg. Indeed, at the turn of the century, *Kleindeutschland*, a neighborhood below 14th Street, would have ranked as the third largest city in Kaiser Wilhelm II's German Empire. The incredible diversity of races, cultures, and languages on the crowded streets of lower Manhattan was captured in print by the young radical John Reed, who wrote about his experiences just before World War I in his adopted land:

New York was an enchanted city to me. I wandered about the streets, from the soaring imperial towers of downtown, along the East River docks, smelling of spices and the clipper ships of the past, through the swarming East Side, alien towns within alien towns, where the smoky glare of miles of clamorous pushcarts made a splendor of shabby streets. I knew Chinatown and Little Italy, Sharkey's and McSorley's saloons, the Bowery lodging houses and the places where the tramps gathered in winter, the Haymarket, the German village and the dives of the Tenderloin. The girls that walked the streets were friends of mine, and the drunken sailors from the world's end. I knew how to get dope, where to go to hire a man to kill an enemy. Within a block of my house was the adventure of the world. Within a mile was every foreign country.

Quite simply, in terms of size and diversity, humankind had never seen anything like New York in the first decade of the twentieth century.

Second, Gotham was rich. Although filled with millions of impoverished immigrants who lived in airless tenements on the Lower East Side, what made Manhattan different from other places in 1909 was the incredible concentration of wealth in the area. At the turn of the twentieth century, for example, approximately half of all the millionaires in the United States, and perhaps a third of those in the entire world, lived in the New York metropolitan area, most of them along Fifth Avenue. And among them were the richest New Yorkers—the men who made the era famous—including John D. Rockefeller, Andrew Carnegie, Henry Clay Frick, August Belmont, Jacob Schiff, and J. P. Morgan, not to mention the Astors and the Vanderbilts.

Third, New York was overwhelming in its density. Whereas London, Paris, Tokyo, and Berlin spread horizontally, Manhattan was the quintessential skyscraper city, a place where real estate was so expensive that the only place to go was up. Even in 1909, tall office buildings were commonplace in the Wall Street financial district, and tens of thousands of white-collar clerical employees were already riding elevators to work in artificially lit places where hundreds of other people were engaged in similar routines.

Fourth, New York was different from other world cities in 1909 because it was a commercial entrepôt rather than a national capital. Since its beginnings in the 1620s, Manhattan had been a place of exchange rather than the meeting place of parliaments and congresses. At the turn of the century, the Port of New

York was not only the busiest and most important in the world, but it was also larger and busier than all other American ports *combined*. In fact, there was no federal income tax in 1909; the federal government operated on import duties collected in the great harbor where the Hudson River meets the Atlantic Ocean.

Finally, New York was a different kind of city in 1909 because its infrastructure was of a size and quality that was unmatched even in Germany, which was then at the height of its power and significance. Gotham's magnificent Croton Aqueduct, opened in 1842, was an international model in terms of water quality and quantity. And New York's public transportation system—steam railroad commuter trains, electric streetcars, and elevated trains—was the most extensive and efficient on earth. Similarly, its subway system, although not as old as those of London (1863), Glasgow (1886), Budapest (1896), Boston (1897), Paris (1900), and Berlin (1902), was by 1909 easily the busiest and most advanced anywhere. New York was a city on the move, and its transit infrastructure was both a cause and a symbol of that phenomenon.

If the glittering Metropolis at the mouth of the Hudson River was a place of confidence and promise in 1909, so also was New York State as a whole. During the colonial period, and indeed as late as 1800, Pennsylvania, Virginia, and Massachusetts had been the dominant jurisdictions in America. Over the course of the nineteenth century, however, and especially after the opening of the Erie Canal in 1825, New York surged ahead of its rivals, and by 1909 it led the nation in population, wealth, manufactures, and electoral votes. Its cities were both prosperous and numerous, and nine of them then ranked among the nation's 100 largest municipalities. In addition to New York City, these were Buffalo, Rochester, Syracuse, Albany, Yonkers, Utica, Schenectady, and Troy.

Obviously, New York City and State had much to celebrate in 1909. Demographically, economically, politically, and culturally, they dominated the nation at the start of the twentieth century. But as Kate Johnson demonstrates so persuasively in *The Hudson-Fulton Celebration: New York's River Festival of 1909 and the Making of a Metropolis*, residents of the Empire State felt overshadowed by their presumably more historic and sophisticated rivals to the north and south. They needed reassurance; they needed their own versions of Patrick Henry, Benjamin Franklin, and Paul Revere. They wanted to establish the fact, or be told of the fact, that New York also had a long and distinguished history and that Empire State residents could take justifiable pride in a long and glorious past.

It should not surprise us, therefore, that civic leaders found something to celebrate in 1909. They used parades, electric light displays, airplane flights, and naval extravaganzas to remind everyone that New York was on the cusp of becoming the greatest city in the world and that the state was the most influential in the Republic. They were caught up in an international mania for world's fairs, and they wanted to use the Hudson-Fulton Celebration to call attention to their skyscrapers, infrastructure, and cultural institutions. Civic leaders wanted to assert that Gotham offered an aesthetically pleasing, workable, and efficient model for other places to emulate. They believed that an appreciation of New York's past among its immigrant citizenry was an effective way to assure political and

Advertisement, *The New York Times*, August 18, 1909

social stability. Using the example of historical figures and events drawn from New York's past, they wanted to unite a diverse population and encourage their participation in mainstream politics and their acceptance of an American way.

But why commemorate a commemoration in 2009? What can we learn from a celebration so long past? First, this book provides an invaluable window on how New York self-consciously and publicly transformed itself from simply a big city to *the* world Metropolis. Second, it is fascinating to consider the subjects of the Celebration itself. The organizers recognized that New York was diverse, and therefore they featured the Indians, the Dutch, and the Germans in their great commemoration. But New York in 1909 was even more an Irish, Italian, and Jewish city, and those groups were hardly to be found in the officially choreographed events of that year. Finally, it is interesting to consider the subjects of remembrance themselves. While Henry Hudson and Robert Fulton might or might not be the dynamic historical figures the world would single out today for collective or instructive celebration, individuals and events from New York's past still possess the power to capture our imagination.

Kate Johnson's *The Hudson-Fulton Celebration* reminds us that not all of the concerns of 1909 were our concerns, but that a business and cultural elite in 1909 could make one version of the past accessible to the masses. Her approach is integrative. By including a variety of voices, she represents the breadth of perspectives found in New York a century ago. Using the abundant record of newspapers, manuscripts, artifacts, and photographs, she weaves together the history of the built environment, the natural landscape, and material culture to provide us with a new lens with which to examine identity in the world's most complex place.

The Hudson-Fulton Celebration grows from Historic Hudson Valley's sixty-year-long commitment to scholarship, programming, and preservation. The largest cultural institution in suburban Westchester County, it administers a network of historic landmarks, including Philipsburg Manor, Van Cortlandt Manor, Montgomery Place, Sunnyside, the Union Church, and the great Rockefeller estate at Pocantico Hills known as Kykuit. The 1909 Celebration and the historical events upon which it was based were important milestones for the city and the region, and provide us, thanks to this book, with a rare opportunity to understand the rich history of the great Metropolis and of the Hudson River Valley.

Kenneth T. Jackson

Jacques Barzun Professor of History and Social Sciences and
Director of the Herbert H. Lehman Center for American History,
Columbia University

1909

HUDSON FULTON CELEBRATION

BATTERY AND CASTLE GARDEN, 1807

WEST POINT, 1790

FIRST SETTLERS OF AMERICA

HENDRIK

DIEDRICH KNABE 1ST VICE PREST.
GEO. H. WEHRENBERG 2ND VICE PREST.

JOHN RIEFE, PRESIDENT.
WM. P. PRINCKHOFF. SEC. & TREAS.

Consumers' Brewing Co.
OF NEW YORK, LTD.
Ave. A, 54 TO 55TH STREETS.
NEW YORK CITY.
TRIPLE-X-COLUMBIA-REAL AMERICAN.
TELEPHONE 860 PLAZA.

NEW YORK HARBOR

OLD DUTCH COLONY OF NEW AMSTERDAM

STATUE OF LIBERTY

Introduction

"To tie up the present to the past we make use of the well known formula that modern New York is foreign in aspect but American in thought and aspiration. How else can we preserve our historic pride? . . . As long as the Metropolis is true to the essentials of democracy, she cannot be stripped of her American character. Superficially, New York is less American than Philadelphia, or even Boston. But we are more American than many a city less tinged with Europe, in our restiveness under misgovernment, in our dealing with large problems in a large way, . . . and even our assumption, so irritating to our neighbors, that we are about the only thing on the continent that counts."

The Evening Post, October 2, 1909

Nineteen hundred and nine marked the year of the history carnival in the United States. From Seattle to Springfield, from San Francisco to New York, Americans mounted elaborate commemorative celebrations as a way to negotiate a period of swift social, political, and technological change.[1] The country was growing more urban, industrial, populous, and ethnically diverse. Graft and corruption were causing a loss of faith in the political system. As electric lights, telephones, automobiles, cameras, and even zippers changed the patterns and rhythm of daily life, Americans looked to the past for answers and inspiration. Through these celebrations, they expressed pride of place and engaged in regional rivalries. The Hudson-Fulton Celebration, an expansive festival centered in New York City and the Hudson Valley, possessed a culturally pluralistic and international character. Civic leaders used the festival to proclaim that New York City had arrived as a world capital and the United States as a world power. A national and international audience took notice as New Yorkers strutted their stuff from New York Harbor to the Erie Canal during this two-week-long event.

Cartoon in the *New York Herald*, September 18, 1909

FALL IN LINE.

Lantern slide of the *Half Moon*

Spectators watching Naval Parade

In this stereoscope card, sightseers on an excursion steamer cheer American warships.

Officially, the Celebration marked the three-hundredth anniversary of Henry Hudson's fateful voyage up the river that now bears his name as well as the one-hundredth anniversary of Robert Fulton's successful run of a steamship on the same waterway in 1807. In September and October of 1909, millions of city residents and out-of-towners experienced a splendid array of fireworks, concerts,

exhibitions, dedications, and land and water parades. Especially memorable were the warships of the great powers, jaw-dropping airplane flights by Wilbur Wright and Glenn Curtiss, and the boldly beautiful nighttime electric illumination of skyscrapers, bridges, and other structures. Because the record crowds tested the municipal infrastructure—the electrical grid, police and emergency services, and the subway, elevated train, and trolley network—this Knickerbocker holiday confirmed the modernity of New York while simultaneously commemorating its past.

This street-and-river fair prompted a flurry of documentary photography as well as fine, decorative, and commercial art, including tons of imaginative souvenirs. The Celebration Commission may have officially divorced itself from commercialism, but that did not keep enterprising businesspeople from offering "Hudson-Fulton neckties, cigarette cases, scarf pins, beefsteak à la Henry Hudson, Clermont patties, Fulton collars, the 'swagger young man's suit,' with the latest Hudson-Fulton cut, Hudson-Fulton sales at all the department stores, and countless brands of Half-Moon cigars and cigarettes."[2] Not surprisingly, the festivities were both image- and word-driven in

Celebration souvenir plate sold by Higgins & Seiter, New York

Left: **Miniature loving cup**

23

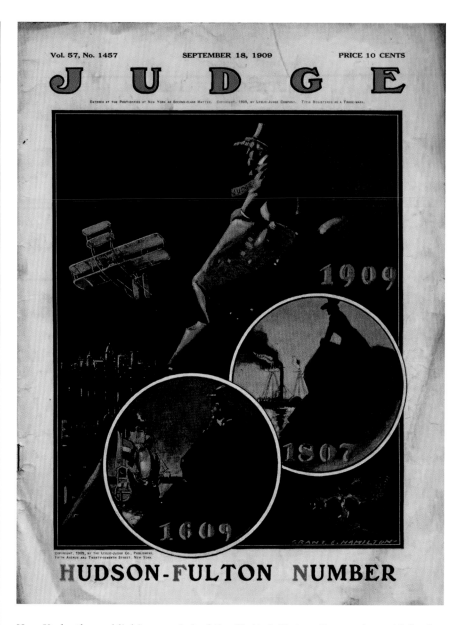

Vol. 57, No. 1457   SEPTEMBER 18, 1909   PRICE 10 CENTS

JUDGE

HUDSON-FULTON NUMBER

**Celebration issue of
Judge magazine**

New York, the publishing capital of the United States. Postcards, guidebooks, and illustrated volumes flooded stores and newsstands. The city's many daily and weekly newspapers put their own particular spin on the happenings. *Judge*, *Scientific American*, and other magazines devoted special issues to the Celebration. Individuals also recorded their impressions of the festivities in diaries, in letters, and on the backs of postcards. The wealth of ephemera, commemorative memorabilia, and documentation makes the festival a rich way to explore the psyche of an era.

The types of activities selected for the Celebration along with the huge amount of attention it generated among New Yorkers help us understand the concerns and interests of a city at a turning point. Ragtime New York was a world quite different from our own, yet some issues are eerily similar—the United States' uncertain standing in a conflict-ridden world, the effect of new technologies on personal and community life, the integration of immigrants, and the resilience and reliability of the city's infrastructure. Just as the citizenry of 1909 looked to the past to deal with social and technological change, twenty-first-century readers can also learn from this celebration.

By 1909, New York had grown into a super-sized urban center. Only eleven years earlier, the independent city of Brooklyn and the four boroughs had consolidated to form the City of New York. With four and one-half million residents, it rivaled—some say surpassed—London as the most populous city in the world. It also possessed the highest ratio of foreign- to native-born residents. One million workers commuted in and out of the city each day. At the time of the Celebration, New York was leading other American cities, including Chicago—its rival for Metropolis status—in the race to build skyscrapers. It was home to the two tallest inhabitable structures in the world, the Metropolitan Life Insurance Tower on Madison Avenue and the Singer Building, now lost, which stood at Liberty and Broadway. In 1909, the city's diverse population, size and scale, and strong embrace of capitalism—symbolized by the Lower East Side, the skyscraper, and Wall Street respectively—were acknowledged internationally as distinctive and modern.[3]

Advertisement, *The New York Times,* August 26, 1909

Souvenir packet of New York views
The Singer Sewing Machine Company published a set of city scenes for tourists attending the Celebration. Between 1908 and 1909, the Singer Building, here pictured with the Half Moon, *had been the tallest skyscraper in the world. However, by the time of the Celebration, New York's Metropolitan Life Insurance Tower had surpassed it.*

Some aspects of the Metropolis would seem familiar to us, others less so. Many classic New York landmarks were in place, or under construction, in 1909. The Statue of Liberty, Brooklyn Bridge, Central Park, Washington Square Arch, and the Custom House (Federal Hall National Memorial) had been joined by Ellis Island's Main Building (1900), the New York Stock Exchange at 18 Broad Street (1903), the Interborough Rapid Transit Corporation's first subway (1904), and the Manhattan and Queensboro Bridges (1909). Warren and Wetmore's Grand Central Terminal and Carrère and Hastings's New York Public Library were in the midst of construction. The Chelsea Piers complex, providing luxurious berths for ocean liners, was nearly complete and parts of it were in operation.

Other features of the city would be less easily recognized. During the heyday of the Manhattan and Brooklyn waterfronts, docks ran for miles along the Hudson and East Rivers. Trolleys and wagons outnumbered automobiles on city streets. Theaters and concert halls dominated New York's cultural landscape, offering vaudeville acts, opera, concerts, lectures, and plays—a few even showed short films. Fun seekers could also visit countless dance halls, saloons, penny arcades, and, on the outskirts of town, amusement parks at Coney Island. In Tin Pan Alley, West 28th Street between Broad-

BROADWAY AND FIFTH AVENUE, NORTH FROM 23D STREET

Two views from the Singer Souvenirs packet

BATHING SCENE AT CONEY ISLAND, NEW YORK'S SUMMER PLAYGROUND

way and Sixth Avenue, music poured out of the windows as sheet music composers including Irving Berlin churned out popular songs.

The front pages of New York's many daily and weekly newspapers offered a glimpse at the landscape of ideas absorbing Americans in the fall of 1909. Many of the popular stories of the day, like the question of whether Robert Peary or Frederick Cook had conquered the North Pole, intersected with the Hudson-Fulton Celebration. These seasoned Arctic explorers set off with their teams on independent ventures in 1907 and 1908 respectively. Although it is now believed that neither of them actually reached the true North Pole, each returned in 1909 to claim that he, and not the other, had done so. Peary and Cook's rival claims and tales of bravery in a strange and unforgiving environment dominated newspapers and magazines, which featured photographs of Inuit people in icy land-

New-York Daily Tribune,
September 12, 1909

One of many newspaper stories about the Peary and Cook controversy, this article featured photographs of Inuits, sled dogs, and the adventurers' wives.

Postcard

Wilbur Wright flying during the Celebration

scapes, smiling husky sled dogs, and American adventurers dressed in arctic attire, including Matthew Henson, Peary's second in command, who was African American. Although the dispute would be settled in Peary's favor to the discredit of Cook, both men were in New York during the Celebration, with Peary's ship *Roosevelt* even joining the great Naval Parade. Reporters reveled in the comparisons between the modern-day adventurers and Henry Hudson, who had repeatedly attempted to sail over the North Pole.[4]

The polar ice cap was not the only frontier recently challenged in 1909. Daredevil aviators took to the sky at European air shows and races. Piloting airplanes and dirigibles, they flirted with death as the world watched. Riveting photographs of burning and crashed aircraft lured readers in with their depictions of tragedy. New Yorkers found these experiments in flight tremendously exciting at a time when most Americans had never seen an airplane in person. As part of the tribute to transportation innovation, Wilbur Wright and Glenn Curtiss would be circling around New York during the Celebration.[5]

Newspapers were also tracking a heated national controversy over environmental conservation and government ethics. Gifford Pinchot, a popular conservationist and head of the Forest Service, had charged Secretary of the Interior Richard Ballinger with betraying the public's trust by allowing private companies access to coal fields on public land in Alaska. President William Howard Taft unwittingly drew even more attention to the clash when he visited the Alaska-Yukon-Pacific Exposition in September 1909.[6] Americans' growing interest in designating lands as protected parks played out in the dedication of the Palisades Interstate Park as part of Celebration festivities.

Political activities leading up to the 1909 fall elections in New York were as lively as they had ever been. Party bosses and faithful met to determine slates of candidates for offices that included the mayor. The city's current mayor, George B. McClellan, Jr., son of the famous Civil War general, would not be running again. Put in office by the Democratic Party's Tammany Hall, he had separated himself from the infamous political machine when he pursued a series of reforms. He was not alone in his disdain for Tammany and the corruption it represented. The "Fusion" cross-party coalition composed of Progressive Republicans, some Labor Party members, independents, and others joined forces to unseat Tammany politicians. A number of Hudson-Fulton Celebration organizers—Seth Low, Herbert Parsons, and Robert de Forest among others—were so-called Fusionists and their names were floated in the press as potential candidates. In the opinion of Charlie Murphy and other Tammany leaders, these do-gooders could ruin a good thing.[7]

"I WON'T SAY WHO SWALLOWED MY POCKETBOOK BUT DON'T LET IT HAPPEN AGAIN"

Cartoon of the Tammany Tiger and Father Knickerbocker in the *New York Herald*, September 29, 1909

Many of the Hudson-Fulton Celebration bigwigs were progressive, either in political affiliation, personal outlook, or both. Their moralistic, pragmatic approach affected the concept of the Celebration and its roster of programs. Progressives, who were optimists and social engineers at heart, believed that they could remedy society's ills through close study of individual problems, the application of systems, and honest work. They created baselines for measuring advancement, favoring numbers and statistics as a concise way to measure success and impact. (To document their work mounting the two-week Celebration, they published an official report that ran 1,421 pages!) The progressive platform stood for clean government, environmental conservation, consumer protection, and prohibition. Progressives sought a business-friendly, strongly centralized government as a way to offer stability to a rapidly changing society and encouraged new Americans to do the same.[8]

Governor Hughes and Celebration officials arriving by boat in Albany

Official banquet at the Hotel Astor

The official banquet was an exclusively male affair, but women were allowed to hear the after-dinner speeches if they sat in the balcony.

There was little diversity among the organizers of this multicultural festival. With rare exception, the 1,500 members of the Celebration Commission were established elites—Anglo-American, male, Christian, and financially comfortable. They allowed ethnic, political, and social clubs to participate, but within strict limits. Their overriding attitude: "we make, you take." A case in point was the scheduling of the Celebration's opening festivities on Yom Kippur, the most solemn religious holiday in the Jewish calendar. Although the president of the Commission ultimately apologized a few days later, this unfortunate event did not speak well for the organizers' attitude toward inclusiveness.[9]

The organizers set forth four goals: to mount an educational rather than commercial celebration, to encourage interest in New York history throughout the state, to facilitate the assimilation of immigrants, and to advance international friendship.[10] With goal number one in mind, organizers created message-filled parades, museum exhibitions, lectures, and student activities inside and outside of the classroom rather than the more typical world's fair promotion of businesses and merchandise. Organizers were pushing history, not consumer goods, and their focus on educational opportunities spoke to their aspirations.

This emphasis on instruction supported the organizers' second goal. During an era when Americans were enchanted with all things colonial, Americans viewed New York as less grounded in the past, and therefore less respectable, than other eastern seaboard states, causing boosters to urge a greater appreciation of the Empire State's history. Progressive-minded organizers also wanted to demonstrate how far New York had come since its founding. In particular, they wanted city residents to understand that they were better off in 1909 than in earlier times, thanks in part to municipal initiatives. And they believed that a historical awakening could build unity among all New Yorkers, whether they were downstaters or upstaters, poor or well off, descendants of colonials or first-generation Americans.

Third, organizers saw the Celebration as a way to help acculturate new Americans. With immigration at record levels during this era, there was concern about the assimilation of recent arrivals into American society. Between the 1880s and the first decade of the 1900s there had been a dramatic shift in immigration trends. In 1907, for example, there were nearly twice as many immigrants entering the country as there had been twenty-five years before. On April 17 of that year, 11,747 immigrants were processed on Ellis Island, a record number for a single day. Many hailed from southern and eastern Europe and therefore seemed more foreign to "old Americans" than the immigrants from northern

and western Europe who had come to the United States in the nineteenth century. Celebration organizers considered history a powerful teaching tool for newcomers. Events from New York's past not only exemplified the principles that underscored democratic government in the United States, but also illustrated how American culture owed a debt of gratitude to, yet was distinct from, Europe's culture. They believed that New York's longstanding multicultural character could offer newcomers a sense of belonging. In the progressive mindset, if new Americans felt a kinship with New York's past, they would be more likely to become involved in mainstream politics and be less susceptible to socialist and anarchist ideologies.[11]

Immigrants registering
This 1890 image shows newcomers passing through the Barge Office, the predecessor to Ellis Island's Main Building.

"The Red Flag in New York"
Frank Leslie's Illustrated Newspaper *showed police breaking up a workers' rally in Tompkins Square in an issue dated January 31, 1874.*

Sailors holding bell from the original *Clermont*

The fourth goal—to encourage understanding among nations—was expressed in an odd way. Rather than build pavilions, participating nations sent warships, an irony noted by social commentators at the time. This was an era when countries expressed international muscle through their navies. Indeed, earlier in 1909, the United States' own flotilla of warships, called the Great White Fleet, had returned from a year-long tour of foreign ports, a thinly veiled expression of world power ambition. Deterring war through military build-up—a contested notion Fulton had advanced a century earlier when peddling his maritime weapons to France and England—was the leitmotif for this international get-together. As political and military tensions grew in Europe prior to World War I, New York offered itself as a peaceful meeting place.

The Hudson-Fulton Celebration evolved from impulses that took years to coalesce into action. The first suggestion for such a commemoration appeared in a letter to the *New-York Tribune* in 1893, when J. H. Suydam wrote that Henry Hudson's sail was worthy of a fête similar to that of the World's Columbian Exposition in Chicago. During the earliest years of the twentieth century, several committees formed to memorialize Hudson or Robert Fulton and their upcoming anniversaries. In April 1906, the governor of New York signed the legislation creating the Hudson-Fulton Celebration Commission. The group immediately began planning for an event in the fall of 1909 that would direct attention to both Hudson and Fulton. To mount the Celebration, they also began raising the million dollars required for such a celebration from New York State, New York City, and individual sponsors large and small.[12]

The Hudson-Fulton Celebration organizers took inspiration from a wide range of public festivals. They looked back to world's fairs held in Philadelphia (1876), Chicago (1893), Paris (1900), Buffalo (1901), and St. Louis (1904). They borrowed ideas and personnel from New Orleans' Mardi Gras carnival. They understood the attractiveness of political, labor, and ethnic pride parades, part of the New York street scene since the colonial period. They watched as an era of anniversary mania swept in with the twentieth century. For example, in 1907 alone, history lovers had begun construction of the Pilgrim Memorial, mounted the Jamestown Exposition to honor the Virginia settlement's founding in 1607, and hosted the Founders' Festival in Philadelphia. This flurry of commemoration undoubtedly raised the stakes for New York's leaders and encouraged them to pursue their own historical tribute.

Crowd in Riverside Park at 108th Street

The Hudson-Fulton Celebration ran from Saturday, September 25, through Monday, October 11. The first half of the Celebration focused on Manhattan, and the second on Brooklyn, the other boroughs, and towns upriver. Four massive parades, one on water and three on land, launched the festivities. On opening day, the inaugural Naval Parade consisting of replicas of Henry Hudson's *Half Moon* and Robert Fulton's *Clermont* and an accompanying flotilla paid tribute to the ten miles of warships anchored in the Hudson River. Three days later, the History of New York Parade or "Great Historical Pageant," designed to capture the spirit of the Celebration as a whole, featured a cavalcade of floats depicting scenes plucked from the Empire State's past. The Military Parade—with its pha-

Washington taking the oath of office at Federal Hall.
The structure is a reproduction of the historic portico

The storming and recapture of Stony Point by
Wayne in July, 1779—a graphic representation

A group of Onondaga Indians—one of the
most picturesque groups in the pageant

Float showing old-time methods of punish-
ment—the ducking-stool, stocks, pillory, etc.

The destruction of the statue of George III. in Bowling Green, New York, by Revolutionary patriots

A section of the huge crowd which lined the route of the pageant. The view is from Twenty-third Street and Fifth Avenue

THE HISTORY OF NEW YORK ON WHEELS

Floats in History Parade
Harper's Magazine *of*
October 9, 1909, included
extensive coverage of the
Celebration's processions.

lanxes of sailors, marines, soldiers, and marching bands—followed two days
after that. The Celebration in Manhattan culminated with the Carnival Parade,
a theatrical nighttime procession akin to Mardi Gras. Each parade took the
same six-mile route starting at 110th Street and Central Park West, snaking
south and east along Central Park to Fifth Avenue, pausing at the Court of
Honor reviewing stand located between 42nd and 40th Streets, and then south
to Washington Square. Each attracted millions of spectators.

Interspersed among the parade spectacles were themed days of accolades and activities, including Worship Day, General Commemoration Day, and Children's Day. Highlights included the official reception at the Metropolitan Opera House of dignitaries such as Japanese Prince Kunihoshi Kuni and Julia Ward Howe, who read a poem she had penned especially for the occasion; the official banquet, also with oratory galore, at the Hotel Astor; the dedication of the Pal-

West Point band and cadets at the Court of Honor
Charles R. Lamb designed this official parade reviewing area.

Banquet favor and interior of lid

isades Interstate Park, the Stony Point Park arch, a monument to Henry Hudson at Spuyten Duyvil, and other memorials; aquatic sports and races for visiting sailors and others on the Hudson; German and Irish music festivals; and parades and pageants mounted by thousands upon thousands of city school children. Residents of the boroughs enjoyed their own receptions, parades, and concerts as well.

On September 29, the *Half Moon* and the *Clermont* sailed northward, setting in motion a whole other roster of events that played out along the Hudson's shores during the second half of the Celebration. Parade floats that had first appeared in Manhattan were disbursed to smaller parades in cities and towns upriver, where civic leaders presided over banquets and dedicated historical monuments. Saturday, October 9, marked the finale of the Celebration with a full day of activities in Troy and the lighting of a series of signal fires at points along the Hudson River from this city south to Staten Island. Cohoes, north of Troy, provided a gentle conclusion, putting on water and land parades, and hosting dignitaries, on October 10 and 11.

While ostensibly mounted to mark seminal events that had occurred centuries before, the Hudson-Fulton Celebration clearly expressed its progressive organizers' current concerns, hopes, and dreams. It allowed them to take measure of themselves, their emerging Metropolis, and the whole Hudson River Valley. They gazed backward and forward while asserting prominence on a national and international stage. These progressives used this two-week, 150-mile-long "block party" to express pride of place and faith in the future while also attempting to address significant challenges. They wanted to test various aspects of their mega-city and its residents. New York stood as a financial, commercial, and publishing behemoth, but did it rate as the Metropolis of the Western Hemisphere, outpacing Chicago or any other city? Was its historical, artistic, and cultural legacy impressive enough? ❖

Ossining schedule of events

opposite: **Map of the Hudson River Valley**
Published in 1909 to coincide with the Celebration, this two-part map showed the areas settled by the Delaware, the Wappingers, and other Native Americans at the time of Hudson's voyage. Modern-day towns and cities, the sites of Celebration festivities, were also picked out on the map.

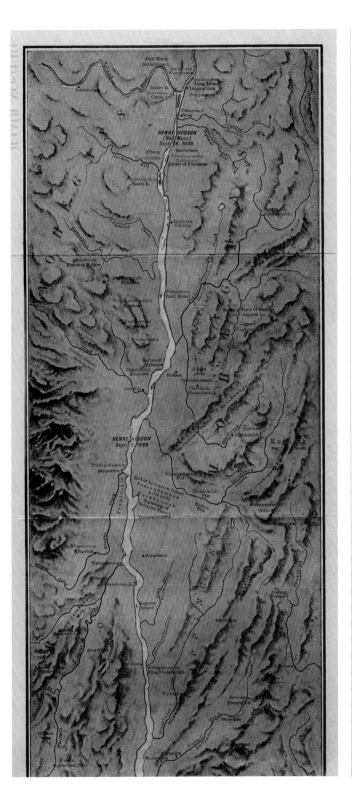

1609
THE HUDSON RIVER
(CAHOHATATEA)
AT THE
TIME OF ITS DISCOVERY BY HENRY HUDSON

By TOWNSEND MAC COUN

AUTHOR OF HISTORICAL GEOGRAPHY CHARTS OF THE UNITED STATES,
HISTORICAL GEOGRAPHY CHARTS OF EUROPE, THE HOLY LAND IN GEOGRAPHY AND HISTORY

The Indian names are obtained from the Dutch Colonial Records; the deeds and patents of the
Van Rensselaer, Schuyler, Livingston, Van Cortlandt, and Philipse families.

As the spelling of Indian names differs greatly the earlier forms have been generally adopted.

Police controlling Celebration spectators

A Test of the
Modern Metropolis

"Records Made Here in Handling Crowds / City Traffic Lines, Railways, Police, and Hotels Show Their Great Efficiency / About 2,000,000 Visitors / Singular Absence of Accidents and No Serious Overcrowding During the Big Celebration"

The New York Times, October 4, 1909

It may seem strange that New York's civic leaders would use a history fair to champion modernity, but such was the case with the Hudson-Fulton Celebration. The festival provided a milestone for measuring the city. Celebration organizers believed that, by looking backward, the people of New York, the United States, and even the world could appreciate the strides the city had made during its relatively short life. Members of the Hudson-Fulton Commission wanted to prove that, even when faced with the additional pressures posed by the Celebration, this huge city could function with efficiency and relative grace. They also wanted to draw attention to the modern cityscape with its magnificent skyscrapers, elegant series of bridges, and new kind of transcendent beauty. This was a chance to test the Metropolis and its varied aspects—municipal services, utilities, mass transportation, and other urban essentials.

Organizers knew from the start that the scope of the affair would challenge the city's inner workings. The effort to finance, plan, and execute the event took the form of a joint public-private initiative, a type of partnership that was growing more common at the turn of the twentieth century as large cities undertook highly disruptive, technologically challenging, and capital-intensive improvements. When planning the Celebration, governmental and business leaders worked together to assure the safety and comfort of the millions expected to attend. As it turned out, in the fall of 1909, over one million out-of-towners poured into New York City, joining four and one-half million city dwellers in the festivities.

Progressive Celebration organizers used a corporate model for organizing their work. They sought the efficiencies offered by a well-run bureaucracy. Like the interconnected departments in a corporation, a network of fifty-one committees managed various aspects of Celebration planning and execution. The Com-

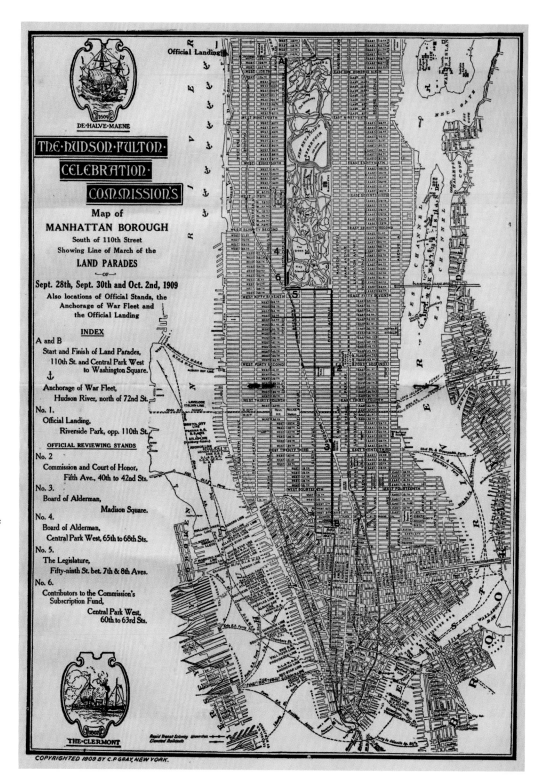

Map of Manhattan noting the location of Celebration events

mission's accountants had a heyday as they meticulously logged funds received and expended and tallied attendance at various events. They generated elaborate sets of statistics, favoring facts and figures over words to express public impact and success. Indeed, records set during the Celebration were cited as benchmarks for years afterward. Even historians were not immune to this quantitative approach. For example, in one official publication, the Celebration's chief historian Edward Hagaman Hall included a short essay entitled "An Estimate of Fulton's Genius," in which he calculated the number of people served and money made by the steamship and ferry lines working in the greater New York area since Fulton launched the *Clermont* in 1807. Before, during, and after the Celebration, organizers relied on press agents to position the Celebration in the best possible light. Entities ranging from the police department to the Interborough Rapid Transit Company also took advantage of the positive public relations opportunities the Celebration offered. New York's many newspaper reporters, as well as members of the international press, were partners in this effort to show that New York had not grown too big for its breeches.[1]

Officials were particularly concerned about controlling and protecting the attending throngs. New York's police were accustomed to handling big crowds, but the Celebration's numerous large-scale events, huge influx of out-of-town visitors, and presence of foreign dignitaries added a new level of complexity.[2] Those in charge of public safety did not have to look far to find troubling reminders of what could go wrong. In 1901, at Buffalo's Pan-American Ex-

Cartoon in *Puck Magazine* (1909)
Newspaper reporters and photographers eagerly chase Henry Hudson's ghost during the Celebration.

Huge crowd in Riverside Park
Sightseers swarmed the east bank of the Hudson River to watch the Naval Parade.

position, a deranged gunman had assassinated President William McKinley. In 1904, a fire aboard the excursion ship *General Slocum* in the East River resulted in the deaths of more than 1,000 adults and children. A few days before the start of the Hudson-Fulton festivities, a week-long series of nighttime carnival parades at Coney Island was marred by runaway horses that caused the death of two policemen and by a gang who pushed their way through the crowd of 300,000 revelers, rubbing women's faces with confetti mixed with burrs and smashing men's straw hats.[3] Mounting as massive and complicated an event as the Hudson-Fulton Celebration was not without risk.

Realizing that the success of the Celebration depended on an effective police force, those in charge of logistics conceived of the department as "a mighty human machine," going so far as to draft blueprints to diagram deployment. For the duration of the Celebration, eighteen-hour shifts were the norm and police were required to stay at the station even when off-duty. In preparation for the event, they received additional training in maintaining a courteous attitude and limiting the use of night sticks.[4]

Police at work during the Celebration

Before and during the event, the police department publicized its crime-fighting tactics. Newspaper stories outlined how plainclothes detectives, uniformed officers, and decoys were watching for thieves at train stations, in hotel lobbies, and on the street. In an effort to simultaneously assure the public while scaring the criminal element, police revealed how they would preemptively round up pickpockets. In their scheme, detectives would trail suspects and force them to inadvertently bump into other pedestrians. This collision would provide the pretense for a charge of disorderly conduct. It was then on to night court for the accused, where they would be remanded to the work house for the duration of the Celebration, a legally questionable but apparently effective approach.[5]

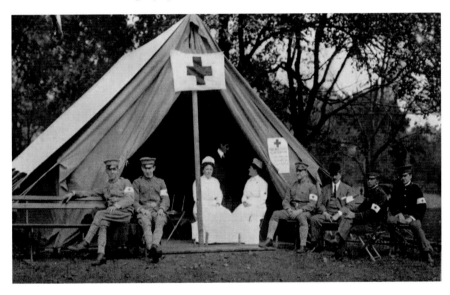

Public health hospital tent open during the Celebration

With lower-than-usual crime and death rates and few serious accidents or complaints of police roughness, municipal leaders saw the successful management of the Celebration as a confirmation of the police department's competence. Stellar sets of statistics were further validated by glowing newspaper articles containing affirmation from guest authorities. What higher tribute could there have been than for visiting German officers to praise New York's policemen as "efficient" and "superb"?[6]

The Celebration's committee of public health and convenience collaborated with the police department and officials to help visitors negotiate the city's intricacies. The committee established a network of information centers, mobile medical units, public toilets, and rest stations. It also distributed an official booklet filled with all kinds of helpful information including legal cab and carriage rates, locations of hospitals and police stations, and directions to Celebration events.[7]

Correspondence from New York's San Remo Hotel

Hotel Astor, located on Broadway at Longacre (Times) Square, decorated for the Celebration

New York Central Lines train schedule

This committee also addressed the additional demand for overnight accommodations. Prior to the event, home and boarding house owners with extra room were encouraged to advertise in one of the city's many daily newspapers. The committee's booklet provided a long list of hotels and boarding houses. On the high end, in an effort to attract a well-heeled clientele, the Hotel Astor, the Plaza, and the Hotel Knickerbocker publicized the names of foreign dignitaries and other celebrities staying at their establishments as well as the details of lavish decorations mounted especially for the event. Although newspapers like the *New York Herald* stated that, during the Celebration, hotel proprietors were forced to put up overflow guests on cots in corridors and had turned away thousands more, reports later indicated that expensive hotels had not been full and that the scarcity of rooms had been erroneously reported in the media.[8]

Moving millions of people to, from, and around the city was a challenge welcomed by transportation companies. In the months and weeks leading up to the Celebration, railways announced that huge numbers of travelers from all over the nation would be heading to New York. Lines of ferries and river steamships—the latter called day liners because they could run from Albany to New York in less than a day—carried merrymakers to the big city. While automobile rental companies offered Maxwells, Ramblers, and Pope-Toledos for hire during the event, most participants used the well-developed system of mass transit to move around town.[9]

All transportation companies associated themselves with this salute to the history of travel, but none was more successful than the Interborough Rapid Transit Company in exploiting the connection. The IRT offered free passes to foreign sailors, thus encouraging the curious to ride on its elevated and subway lines while also receiving favorable press for this hospitable gesture. Since its two subway lines, running from City Hall to the Bronx and from Manhattan to Brooklyn, had opened only recently—in 1904 and 1908 respectively—many out-of-towners experienced underground travel for the first time. Newsflashes in the city's many daily papers documented record ridership on the subway and elevated lines. Records set during the Celebration included the IRT's single busiest day up to that point, September 30, with 2,157,989 passengers served; fifteen million riders accommodated in an eight-day period; and $750,000 in income earned during the same stretch. As a result, the value of stock shares in the Interborough-Metropolitan lines rose during the Celebration and $25,000 was distributed among the employees in gratitude for their outstanding work. The level of achievement reached during the Hudson-Fulton Celebration would not be surpassed for years, and proved beyond a doubt the efficiency of New York's mass transit system.[10]

Postcard of the *Robert Fulton*, a steamer built for the Celebration

Postcard of the City Hall subway station

The *Clermont*, Rookwood Pottery tiles, IRT Fulton Street station (1905)

The Celebration spotlight also shone brightly on municipal maintenance workers. Not only did they prepare the city prior to the Celebration so that it looked its best, but they also dealt with the destruction and debris left in the wake of massive crowds. For example, the day after the Hudson River Naval Parade, staff began to replant acres of grass and to repair and replace fences at Riverside Park, damaged by the millions of spectators who had gathered there to view the festivities. Street cleaning crews, referred to as the "White Wings," picked up trash before, during, and after the parades. Among the largest pieces of detritus were soapboxes, wooden crates strong enough to stand on, that parade spectators had purchased from street vendors to achieve a better vantage point. To keep street cleaners' morale high, the commissioner of the department designated two parade grandstands for the families of workers and their off-duty comrades, an act that bolstered personal and civic pride among those who felt that they were at the bottom of the municipal ladder and constantly disparaged.[11]

Like tidy streets, affordable tickets to grandstand seating came to symbolize good government during the Celebration. Reform Republicans dominated the Commission, and they were particularly anxious to mount a model event free of corruption. This sentiment even extended to bleachers. In an attempt to distribute

White Wings in *Munsey's Magazine* (1900)

In the 1890s, Commissioner George Waring organized the department of street cleaners in military fashion, issuing white uniforms that prompted the distinctive nickname.

Parade grandstand on Central Park West

tickets fairly and to keep construction costs down, the organizers came up with a system that allowed clubs and charitable groups to apply for city permits to build grandstands, many of which were located in Central Park along the parade route on Central Park West. According to the permit agreement, organizations would pay for the construction of their stands outright, but could cover costs through ticket sales to their members. This strategy was designed to both keep the Commission's construction costs to a minimum and to get tickets into the hands of spectators without the interference of speculators and scalpers. When one group ran afoul of their permit, newspapers covered the episode with glee. Investigators discovered that scalpers had gotten their hands on tickets for bleachers built by the Founders and Patriots of America. Further digging revealed that the Secretary General of this august organization had paid the contractor in tickets rather than cash. In response, a furious Parks Commissioner Henry Smith launched a dramatic raid at four o'clock in the morning, resulting in the city-ordered destruction of the stands within a few hours. The whole affair was particularly embarrassing because a number of Celebration organizers were members of the offending organization. Smith's swift retribution represented the anti-graft thrust of the Celebration.[12]

Plaza Hotel

On a happier note were the thrilling nighttime illuminations mounted by electric power companies, perhaps the most successful part of the Hudson-Fulton Celebration. While the exhibition grounds of the 1893 Chicago World's Fair and 1901 Buffalo Pan-American Exposition had featured exterior lighting displays, the Hudson-Fulton show was more spectacular, ambitious, and intriguing because it took place throughout the city and celebrated city landmarks, old and new. This demonstration permitted Celebration organizers to achieve their dream of putting the cityscape on exhibition while also allowing utility companies to promote the efficacy of electrical power.

New York had enjoyed a long association with Thomas Edison, the creator of the first commercially viable incandescent lightbulb in 1879, who had developed many of his inventions at his laboratory in nearby Menlo Park, New Jersey. He had established the first central electrical power station in the world on Pearl Street in lower Manhattan in 1883. A few years later, when considering what power source to use for the subway, the IRT's engineers chose direct electrical current as championed by Edison.[13]

By 1909, Gotham's major utility firm, Consolidated Gas, had purchased Edison's first company as well as other independent concerns, uniting them under the umbrella of the New York Edison Company. During the Celebration, this subsidiary launched a clever campaign to help businesses implement artistic exterior electrical displays while also offering lower utility rates to those who decorated with lights. It whipped up interest among New York's citizenry by publicizing the hoopla leading up to the Celebration. Newspapers touted "wonders in lighting" even prior to installation, reporting on how a force of 10,000 workers would be stringing electrical wires for a month before the start of the event. Using undeniable hyperbole, a representative of the Commission crowed that now that the North Pole had been discovered and a man had flown over the English Channel in an airplane, the Hudson-Fulton Celebration would turn night into day. The New York Edison Company also placed a series of visually appealing advertisements in New York newspapers before, during, and after the Celebration that linked Edison's incandescent lightbulb to Fulton's steamship, both revolutionary forms of technology. Some of these ads featured photographs of structures illuminated at night as further proof of this technology's resilience and versatility. The Celebration provided the opportunity for these relatively young utilities to flex their muscles and to prove themselves able to accommodate the extra electrical load. After the event, dazzling facts and figures about electricity circulated, including that the half million or more incandescent bulbs temporarily installed during the festivities resulted in a light measure of four million candlepower. If any doubted the value of nighttime illumination, Mr. Richard Blau, in a classic letter to the editor of *The New York Times*, pointed out that such display was not a waste of

Three Great Lights of Civilization

Hudson flashed his brilliant rays of discovery up and down the Hudson river illuminating the pathway of settlement.

Fulton flashed his inventive brilliancy over the same waters, and made navigation possible, independent of the winds.

Electric light will illuminate the whole scene of Hudson's discovery and Fulton's achievement during the Hudson-Fulton Celebration. Millions of candle power of electric light will turn New York nights into day.

The special rate of 5c. per kilowatt hour on electric light for decorative purposes warrants its most wide public use.

The New York Edison Company

Telephone Worth 3000   55 Duane Street

Advertisement, *The New York Times*, September 8, 1909

Washington Arch

money, but rather provided an opportunity to signal Martians since the orbit of the red planet would bring it near Earth at the time of the Celebration.[14]

By all accounts, the lighting display was spectacular, as thousands of incandescent bulbs lined the six-mile parade route, ornamented the Celebration's pillared Court of Honor adjacent to the New York Public Library, and outlined such landmarks as City Hall, Washington Arch, the Riverside Drive Viaduct, and the four East River bridges, including the brand new Manhattan Bridge. Searchlights shone on the Statue of Liberty and Grant's Tomb. Designers harnessed various forms of lighting to showcase the Metropolitan Life Insurance Tower, the

Three East River bridges during the Celebration

Ornamental architectural lighting offered a new kind of urban beauty.

tallest in the world. When the tower's display was turned on, people stood in Madison Square mesmerized, watching light streaming from every window, the clock face on the twenty-sixth floor glowing, and the golden ball on the top flashing red at the hour and quarter hours. No less a connoisseur than Belle de Costa Greene, J. P. Morgan's curator, who termed the Celebration as a whole "disgusting," confided to Bernard Berenson that she was "perforce amused & a tiny wee bit excited by the electrical display" and that Fifth Avenue was "a fairyland thoroughfare of electric lights." This event made city nights seem magical and further encouraged the association of ornamental lighting with metropolitan status.[15]

General Electric, a company founded by Edison as his research arm, heightened the excitement by mounting twice-nightly light shows on the Hudson River at 155th Street. Lighting designer and engineer William D'Arcy Ryan used his "scintillator" to achieve the effect of the aurora borealis. He and his assistants fitted twenty powerful searchlights with tinted lenses and projected the

The Scintillator at the San Francisco Exposition, 1915

The lightshow William D'Arcy Ryan designed for this world's fair was similar to the one that amazed New Yorkers in 1909.

colorful rays upon a "steam curtain." The curtain was formed by vapors emitted by steam pipes, some of which were one hundred feet high. Smoke bombs set off periodically punctuated the display. Ryan and his men, with the help of steam from two locomotives, also created an illusion of the *Clermont* as a "phantom ship of the sky." Considered an artist with light, Ryan had stunned viewers with his groundbreaking illumination of Niagara Falls in 1907. His artistic light shows at San Francisco's Panama-Pacific International Exposition in 1915 accrued him even greater fame.[16]

Not all statements underscoring the city's modernity were big, bold, and spectacular. Newspapers were full of amusing anecdotes involving out-of-towners during the Celebration. The actions and comments of "Country Cousins"—an affectionate yet pejorative moniker commonly used at the time—illustrated how different life was in the big city. Tricked by a devilish street kid, one Jefferson County man tried to mail a letter in a fire alarm box, causing horse-drawn fire engines to roar to the scene. When spying the subway's tiled walls, a pair of elderly upstate visitors assumed they were in a "dairy lunch" place. One out-of-town visitor was so special that he was interviewed by both the *New York Herald* and *The New York Times*. Having moved to California in 1862, Louis Heller was back in New York for the first time in nearly fifty years. Full of memories, he looked for P. T. Barnum's Wonder Palace in Park Row among other long-gone landmarks. He recalled that when he was last in the city, Union troops were marching toward Civil War battlefields and Central Park was not yet completed. In other ways the typical tourist, this septuagenarian admitted that his neck was sore from looking up at the skyscrapers and counting the number of floors.[17]

During the Hudson-Fulton Celebration, New Yorkers looked backward to create a contrast with modern times. This was important, because they felt as if the whole world were watching the progress of their city. As one editorial put it, it was not a celebration of Henry Hudson or Robert Fulton, but a tribute to New York City that gauged the skills of its civic leaders, the behavior of its citizens, and the performance of urban systems.[18] The city functioned well during the event. There were few serious incidents and no disasters. Police, sanitation, and other municipal departments used their accomplishments to burnish their public image. Companies like the IRT and the New York Edison Company considered their achievements extremely significant, proof that large-scale technologies were reliable, efficient, and essential to modern living. This celebratory experiment yielded overall positive results when testing the capacity of the Metropolis. ❖

Celebration postcard of Manhattan Island before the Dutch

The Quandary of New York History

"The State of New York, when compared with her neighbors on the east and south, has heretofore shown questionable modesty in refraining from exploiting her own history. A glance at the book-shelves of any great public library will show how industrious the historians of Massachusetts and Pennsylvania and Virginia have been in recording the annals of which they are justly proud and how comparatively indifferent our own writers have been in this field. And this disparity has resulted in a very general ignorance of the full part played by our Colony and State in our national history. Furthermore, it has led to a positive and unfortunate misconception by many persons of the dignity of our State history."

Edward Hagaman Hall, *The Hudson-Fulton Celebration 1909*

In 1909, New York suffered from a historically induced inferiority complex. If there had been a contest among the original thirteen colonies as to whose history was the most quintessentially American, New York would have lost hands down. Hudson-Fulton Celebration organizers felt compelled to champion a past held in low regard by professional historians and history enthusiasts alike. Indeed, one of their main goals in mounting the Celebration was to encourage greater interest in New York's history. Their effort was not only driven by pride in their city and state, but also by a belief that an understanding of history informed civic participation and was an important part of the acculturation of all Americans. With limited success, civic leaders looked to the annals of New York history to find a "useable past."

Some critics laid blame for New York's poor historical showing squarely at the feet of Washington Irving (1783–1859). Although the situation was far more complicated, they collared Irving as the villain most culpable. In 1809, Irving, writing under the pseudonym of Diedrich Knickerbocker, had published *A History of New York*, a book that infuriated historians for generations to come. Assuming the persona of an eccentric antiquarian, Irving had incorporated real people and events drawn from New Netherland's past into his comic, fictionalized account.

Portrait of Washington Irving
John Wesley Jarvis painted the young writer in 1809, the year A History of New York *was published.*

53

Comical early New Yorkers
George Cruikshank created this sketch for an edition of A History of New York *published in 1835.*

He cast Peter Stuyvesant, William Kieft, Anthony Van Corlear, and other New Netherland notables as ineffectual bumblers who spent most of their time drinking, smoking, and arguing. Their patron saint, Nicholas, interceded repeatedly to save these seventeenth-century stooges from themselves. In his satire, Irving not only nimbly skewered New York's founders, but also poked fun at contemporary Jeffersonian politics and a then-popular travel guide to New York, thus achieving a triple mock. This brilliant volume dazzled readers, but at a cost to New York's historical image over the long term.[1]

By skillfully and uproariously weaving fact with fiction, Irving made New York's early history his domain. With this book, Irving thrust himself and early New York onto the international stage. The reading public on either side of the Atlantic—including Sir Walter Scott, Samuel Taylor Coleridge, and other literary lions—took notice of his inspired account. Almost immediately, "Knickerbocker" became synonymous with "New Yorker." With the advent of widespread book illustration, Irving's burlesque became even more memorable. Over the years, George Cruikshank, Felix O. C. Darley, Maxfield Parrish, and other graphic artists provided lively illustrations. By 1909, more than ninety editions had been published, not counting translations into French, German, and Swedish. But Irving's success did not bolster New York's standing. Not only was his description of the colony's founding so vivid that for decades afterward readers had trouble conceiving of alternate versions, but it also branded the topic of early New York as the stuff of laughter.[2]

At the time of the Celebration, Irving and *A History of New York* received mixed reviews. In an article in *The Evening Post,* Esther Singleton, who had just published a history of early New York life and material culture, admitted that it was hard to compete with the literary skills of Irving. In the same article, an unidentified historian took a contrary view of the *History,* quipping "few people read it, fewer enjoy it." Jonkheer J. Louden, ambassador from the Netherlands, criticized Irving from the podium throughout the Celebration. Using faint praise, Louden remarked how Irving had depicted seventeenth-century New York with "witty inaccuracy." In a less guarded moment, he fumed that the early writer had "almost made the history of New York ridiculous, but we can stand it." The Celebration's official record noted that the misfortune was not so much with the book's "satire, which any person with a reasonable sense of humor can appreciate, as the period at which it appeared—a period barren of any worthy and serious history of New York. The result was that many persons derived their impressions of the character of the founders of New York from Irving's whimsical misconceptions." In actuality, many New York histories had been produced during the nineteenth and early twentieth centuries yet Irving's book was still popular.[3]

Peter Stuyvesants Army entering New Amsterdam.

New Netherland's first families carrying heraldic emblems
In this fold-out lithograph contained in an 1850 edition of Irving's satire, William Heath depicted New York's founding fathers as buffoons. Images like these contributed to the popular perception of New York's colonial past as laughable.

For all the grumbling about the lack of a serious history, the organizers' attempt to resurrect New York's historical reputation did not extend to the academic arena. They did not commission any new histories. Nor did they choose sides in the then hotly contested debates in New York academic and political circles over the hows and whys of authoring histories and preserving official records. They did not actively support the new "social sciences" approach to history advanced by Columbia University's Charles Beard. For the most part, they were enthusiastic amateurs, not teachers, scholars, or archivists. They believed in the progressive mode so central to nineteenth-century historical writing. In

Oloffe Van Cortlandt's vision

Maxfield Parrish illustrated an edition of A History of New York *published in 1900.*

"*And* Oloffe *bethought him, and he hastened and climbed up to the top of one of the tallest trees, and saw that the smoke spread over a great extent of country; and, as he considered it more attentively, he fancied that the great volume of smoke assumed a variety of marvellous forms, where in dim obscurity he saw shadowed out palaces and domes and lofty spires.*"

their pragmatic way, they wanted to present "the facts of history and of material and social progress."[4]

The trouble was more deep-seated and rested in part with local character. New Yorkers suffered from historical amnesia. Unlike their New England neighbors, they did not possess a deep tradition of documenting and reflecting upon what had been. While the Puritans in Massachusetts were convinced from the start of settlement that they were blazing a virtuous and memorable trail, New York's particulars were different. First and foremost, New Netherland was founded as a corporation, not as a political entity. The colony, and later state, continued to bear this commercial imprint, leading New Yorkers to focus on imminent business prospects rather than past deeds. As early as 1809, Washington Irving recognized New Yorkers' forward outlook. In a futuristic scene in Knickerbocker's *History*, seventeenth-century New Yorker Oloffe Van Cortlandt beholds a vision of the impressive city that little New Amsterdam would become.[5]

There were other reasons not to look back. First off, Dutch was the official language until the colony was taken over by the English in 1664. Although some New Yorkers continued to speak Dutch into the nineteenth century, Anglophone historians were perplexed by records in an antiquated form of the Dutch language. They ignored them until they were translated into English, a process begun in the nineteenth century and one that continues to the present day.[6]

Linguistic difficulty was only part of the trouble. Scholars found New York's past particularly thorny because it did not fit with their concept of appropriate historical subject matter. In contrast to modern historical method, where scholars research the documentary record and then draw conclusions from what they have gleaned, colleges in Europe and the United States at the time taught history students that they should determine their arguments first and then select facts to support their positions. Their passionate arguments should be ennobling to the reader, and offer proof that western civilization was tracking ever upward. Their subject matter should be great men and great events. American historians inserted an additional twist into this formula: they were also intent on proving that the young United States was socially and morally superior to "old Europe." New York's dodgy past ran counter to their argument.

New York's past was not always laudable. When nineteenth-century historians trained in this manner looked backward, they had some trouble positioning the colony in a positive, all-American light. The list of offenses was long. The colony had been founded by a country other than England, making it suspect from the start. When New Netherland surrendered to the English in 1664, it did so without firing a shot, an act viewed by some as cowardly. During the colonial period, New York was famous for tolerating corrupt politicians and pirates. The manorial system that dominated the Hudson Valley, where a few wealthy landowners rented farmsteads to tenants, conflicted with the American desire to own land outright. Perhaps the greatest sin was Manhattan's position during the American War of Independence when it remained loyal to the crown. British troops

Celebration postcard of New York City Hall when occupied by the English

NEW YORK CITY HALL WHEN OCCUPIED BY THE ENGLISH

defeated Washington's soldiers in the Battle of Brooklyn in 1776, and controlled Manhattan until they evacuated late in 1783, making New York the last British stronghold in the rebel colonies. Americans also remembered New York as the place where the British kept patriot soldiers aboard notorious prison ships. The record was so grim that when historian William Dunlap addressed the Revolutionary War in *A History of New York, For Schools* (1837), he turned to stories of New England's patriotic activity rather than focus solely on Manhattan's questionable experiences.[7]

Indeed, stories drawn from the history of New England came to dominate the nation's identity and "old time New England" came to mean "old time America." During the nineteenth century, historians crafted a grand narrative of the nation's beginnings knowing that these stories would represent a shared belief system. Reflective of their time, nineteenth-century Americans appreciated New England's religious founding, Patriot activity during the Revolution, and strong intellectual tradition. The migration of Yankees to other parts of the United States also helped spread fond associations. New England's past offered comforting symbols that filled a psychic void as a growing number of people left farms to work in factories or live in cities. By the end of the nineteenth century, iconic New England images such as Pilgrims, the Minutemen, saltbox farmhouses, and town greens were seen as archetypally American. If only New York could claim this past for its own! One enterprising newspaper reporter tried to do just this when he claimed "it was only the mischance of weather that prevented the Pilgrim fathers from landing at New Amsterdam instead of Plymouth, which would have retarded the settlement and development of New England for probably a century, besides giving New York still more historical importance." A comparison of the creation myths of Boston and Manhattan said it all. Boston stood as the "shining city on the hill," a testament to the Puritans' righteousness, while the tale developed that Peter Minuit bought Manhattan Island from the Lenape for the equivalent of twenty-four dollars in trade goods, the city born of a swindle.[8]

FLOAT — PURCHASE OF MANHATTAN

Postcard of the float representing Minuit's purchase of Manhattan

New York's envy only heightened when it looked at the emblematic figures representing other original colonies. Behold the Puritan, the Quaker, and the Cavalier representing Massachusetts, Pennsylvania, and Virginia respectively, all distinguished personages. No oddballs like

Artist's rendering of the Father Knickerbocker float

Diedrich Knickerbocker or clowns like the Dutchmen in Irving's satire. When organizers lamented the state of New York history, they were, in part, yearning for a noble allegorical figure who was worthy of allegiance to represent New York. During the Celebration, they launched Father Knickerbocker to compete with the Puritan and the Quaker. While this emblematic figure had existed since the 1890s at least, his placement on the culminating float of the History of New York Parade raised his public profile. As depicted on the float, this somber but gentle patriarch possessed an uncanny resemblance to Benjamin Franklin. Like the Statue of Liberty, which would supersede him as the symbol of New York, Father Knickerbocker encouraged unity among people of diverse origins while maintaining a dignified demeanor. Try as the Celebration organizers might to promote him, the figure of Father Knickerbocker did not endure in the public psyche.[9]

While early New York City could not claim the nobility of colonial Philadelphia or Boston, the Hudson River Valley to the north could. Ironically, the Celebration that was meant to show New York City as a contender for world supremacy had to look to the surrounding countryside for its claims to moral greatness, even if its own strides in urban municipal progress were genuinely laudable. The Hudson Valley's important role in the Revolutionary War was New York's saving grace and a convenient connection to the Celebration's Hudson River sailor honorees. Looking beyond New York City's checkered past, tourists from the early nineteenth century onward recognized the Hudson Valley as both

View from Fishkill looking toward West Point

This aquatint appeared in the Hudson River *Portfolio, c. 1825.*

a beautiful and instructive landscape. With approximately one-third of the Revolution's battles fought on or near the Hudson's shores, authors of early guidebooks and travelers' accounts crafted a stock narrative that promoted the Hudson Valley as a crucible of the new republic. British travelers in particular, who had been steeped in the philosophy of Edmund Burke, considered it a perfect example of how beautiful scenery was made all the more noble when consecrated by important human struggle. They likened the Hudson Valley to the Rhine Valley, another picturesque corridor with richly romantic, historical associations. If one wanted to understand what it was to be American, sailing up the Hudson River was, in its own way, like reading a history book.[10] When planning the History of New York Parade, Celebration organizers must have recognized this ritual of consuming New York history as a series of vignettes. In the case of the History Parade, the historical scenes would pass by the spectators rather than the reverse. It is no coincidence that the storming of Stony Point, the capture of Major André, and other events and tales described in Valley guidebooks appeared as floats in the Celebration's History Parade.

By the standards of the turn of the twentieth century—when history was being put to serious social uses—New York's early colonial past came up short, due to historical happenstance as well as to the primacy given to Washington Irving's whimsical version of the story. Colonial New York did not offer the wealth of useful clichés that Boston or Philadelphia did, clichés that suited the values of those who wanted to use history to engineer contemporary social values. This was a disappointment to Celebration organizers who stated that a knowledge of history encourages a "love of country, civic pride, and loyalty to established institutions. It serves to bind a people together, make it more homogenous and give it stability. And it makes the inhabitants better citizens by holding up to their eyes lofty traditions to enlist their affections and inspire their imitation."[11]

FLOAT — STORMING OF STONY POINT

Postcards of floats representing Hudson Valley Revolutionary War scenes

These civic leaders were eager to promote a narrative that challenged Washington Irving's comedic account of early New York. Through Celebration events, particularly the History of New York Parade, they wanted to straighten out the Empire State's misunderstood past and to encourage New York's ever-growing population to focus on the serious and the stirring. In their opinion, the time for laughing was over in 1909. A past in which all could take pride was desperately needed. ❖

FLOAT — CAPTURE OF ANDRÉ

Hudson's Valor, Fulton's Genius

" We celebrate in Hudson the great race of men who made the age of discovery.... We celebrate in Fulton the great race of men whose inventive genius has laid the foundation for a broad, nobler and more permanent civilization the world over."

Senator Elihu Root, Hudson-Fulton Banquet Speech, September 29, 1909

Civic leaders, yearning for heroic and instructive biographies as a source of inspiration and reason for holidaymaking, selected Henry Hudson and Robert Fulton as worthy of accolades. This joint tribute commemorated the three-hundredth anniversary of Hudson's exploits in 1609 and the one-hundredth anniversary of Fulton's feat in 1807. Numerical convergence was important, but it was not the only reason why these men were selected. Hudson and Fulton, each in his own way, represented contemporary hopes and concerns in 1909.

All cultures have heroes, but in the United States they have played a particularly important role. Beginning with the canonization of George Washington as the country's first secular saint, individual accomplishment has been promoted as the essence of the American way. Realizing that the population would be united by ideas rather than cultural origin or religion—and acting on the belief that good Americans were made, not born—parents and teachers from the early national period onward encouraged children to study the lives of famous Americans and to imitate them. They believed that if children absorbed the moral and political lessons contained in these stories, they would grow up to be active and informed citizens and contribute to the longevity of the United States government. To this day, inspirational biographies enjoy a special place on the American bookshelf.

In the early twentieth century, Hudson and Fulton rated as heroes for modern times. According to their Celebration bios, they possessed typically American attributes and their areas of expertise were ones New Yorkers

Celebration postcard

63

Hudson River Day Line schedule

could appreciate in 1909. During this era of invention, Hudson and Fulton were portrayed as full of Yankee ingenuity—even if they were not actually Yankees. They addressed challenges with vigor, experimented with different tacks, and soldiered on despite obstacles. Who could be more relevant than an early explorer and a transportation pioneer in a year when Arctic adventurers and aviators were challenging long-accepted boundaries, their risky exploits splashed all over the newspapers? In this city of steamer captains and sales-men, New Yorkers felt a kinship to men tied to the maritime and mercantile world. In 1909, New York was still a bustling port city, with vast quantities of products and materials arriving daily by boat and millions of people traveling aboard ferries, steamboats, and ocean liners. Similarly, the city's legendary business community could certainly appreciate Hudson's quest for a shorter trade route and Fulton's desire to move goods and people more efficiently.

The pairing of Hudson and Fulton also revealed ambivalence about the role of sophisticated technology that marked modern life. Hudson and his vessel with billowing sails stood as a pre-industrial icon while Fulton and his steam-boat with its belching smokestack symbolized pride in the industrial. The changes associated with such advancements prompted people to cast a wistful look backward to simpler tools and times even as they were taking advantage of new conveniences and purchasing factory-produced goods. The mourning of what was lost—clearly expressed in the arts and crafts and colonial revival movements that romanticized the past—was not confined to New York, but could be seen in industrializing countries throughout the world. A case in point is the prevalence of the sailing ship emblem. While it enjoyed centrality in the design and decorations of New York's 1909 event, it was also a favored motif throughout the United States and Europe.

In their selection of Hudson and Fulton, both British in origin, the organizers signaled another strongly held value. It was no coincidence that Hudson hailed from England and Fulton, of Scotch-Irish extraction, had been born in colonial Pennsylvania. Organizers gave primacy to Anglo-American culture at this multicultural festival, a preference that did not go unnoticed. Passing over Giovanni da Verrazano, an Italian sailing under the French flag who had entered New York Harbor in 1524 nearly one hundred years before Hudson, caused a ruckus. Celebration organizers explained away Verrazano's dismissal by pinning great importance on Hudson's travel to the upper reaches of the navigable part of the Hudson, well beyond New York Harbor which had been the extent of Ver-

Engraving of Giovanni da Verrazano

razano's sojourn. But to Italian Americans the slight was clear. It represented the highly prejudicial climate of the time. During the Celebration festivities, contributions from other nationalities were touched on, but ultimately Anglo-American historical figures and accomplishments dominated.[1]

The attributes assigned to each man were complementary. Hudson stood as the courageous quester while Fulton epitomized the wunderkind artist-engineer. In 1909, New Yorkers anointed Henry Hudson (1570?–1611) as the virile and valiant adventurer who gave the Dutch claim to the land that would later become New Netherland and eventually New York, even though the record documenting his activities was thin. Historians know that Hudson undertook four voyages funded by various companies in search of a shorter trade route to Asia. Laboring under the misconception that the top of the world contained warm, navigable waters, Hudson repeatedly headed toward the upper latitudes in an attempt to break through the polar ice.[2]

Indians greeting Hudson, *McClure's Magazine* (October 1909)

The Dutch East India Company underwrote his third and most famous voyage in 1609. Hudson and his crew set sail aboard the *Half Moon* on March 25. It is assumed that he headed north along the Norway coast until he could go no farther. But instead of returning to the Netherlands as his contract with the East India Company stipulated, he inexplicably headed west to North America, snaking along the coast from Penobscot Bay south to Chesapeake Bay. The *Half Moon* then doubled back to present-day New York Harbor. Between September 3 and October 4, Hudson and his men explored the river now named for him. When the crew reached the area of present-day Albany, a few members set out from the *Half Moon* in a smaller boat to confirm that the ship could not travel beyond this point. They progressed as far as the Waterford area, turned around, and sailed back down the river. As Hudson and *Half Moon* First Mate Robert Juet documented in their journals, the crew made contact with indigenous people many times. Some of these interactions were peaceful and some violent. On his trip to Europe, Hudson put in at an English port, supposedly for rest and supplies, never completing his journey to Amsterdam. Whether the English detained him, or he simply did not want to return to the Netherlands because he had disobeyed orders, he sent his log and charts to the Dutch East India Company. Based on Hudson's exploration of New York Bay and the Hudson River, the Dutch claimed this territory in the name of the Netherlands.[3]

Although he made one more attempt to sail through the polar ice cap, this time underwritten by the English, Hudson never found his fabled water passage. In 1611, his mutinous crew set him, his son, and a handful of sick sailors adrift in a small boat in northern Canada, the last recorded sighting of Hudson and

Celebration postcard of Indians helping Hudson land

Celebration postcard depicting the death of Hudson

THE DEATH OF HUDSON
From the painting by Sir John Collier in the Tate Gallery London, Eng.

his companions. By the time of the 1909 Celebration, Hudson's defeat did not matter. His importance lay in his courage and doggedness. In the eyes of his 1909 champions, his failure was not a liability, but actually made him nobler. This man rated as a "martyr."[4]

In their tributes, Celebration orators crowned Hudson "the great and fearless searcher of unknown lands," "a man of experience, of ardor and of wisdom," "a man who knows no terror, who counts no difficulty too great," and—if that were not enough—"master seaman, brave commander, persistent in every work that was given him to do, faithful to duty even unto death, great discoverer, [and] benefactor of mankind." Above all, his exploration of the Hudson River set the stage for the development of this Metropolis. In their Eurocentric approach to history, Celebration organizers gave Hudson credit for introducing civilization to this part of the "barbarous" New World.[5]

Harper's Weekly,
September 25, 1909
In this whimsical scene, the spirit of Henry Hudson watches Manhattan's 1909 festivities from the heavens.

Hudson made excellent hero material in part because so little was known about him. Not even his likeness existed. With no documentation about his appearance and little about his personality, writers and orators could be expansive and creative. At the time of the Celebration, one journalist claimed that "we know his character by his works." Speechmaker Governor Charles Evans Hughes valued Hudson's qualities "of daring, of unfailing courage, of persistence, of loyalty and of truth," while admitting in the very next sentence "it is to be regretted that we know so little of the great discoverer." Elbert Hubbard surmised that Hudson was "the typical stubborn, freckled, sandy Englishman who never knows when he is whipped."[6] Much earlier, the prescient Washington Irving, writing as Diedrich Knickerbocker, had provided a mock portrait of Hudson for the ages. He was:

A short, square, brawny old gentleman, with a double chin and a mastiff mouth, and a broad copper nose, which was supposed in those days to have acquired its fiery hue from the constant neighbourhood of his tobacco-pipe. . . . He wore a commodore's cocked hat on one side of his head. . . . He was remarkable for always jerking up his breeches when he gave out his orders. . . . Such was Hendrick Hudson about whom we have heard so much and know so little. I have been thus particular in description for benefit of modern painters and statuaries, that they may represent him as he was; and not, according to their common custom with modern heroes, make him look like Caesar, or Marcus Aurelius, or Apollo Belvidere [sic].[7]

Celebration post-card featuring a portrait of Fulton after Benjamin West

Robert Fulton (1765–1815) was less shrouded in mystery, and his story was reminiscent of two archetypes found in juvenile fiction. The first was the character of a poor American orphan boy who gets ahead through his own "pluck and luck," supplemented by the aid of a fatherly benefactor, as depicted in the *Ragged Dick* series (begun in 1867), *Slow and Sure* (1900), *Risen From the Ranks* (1909), and other novels penned by Horatio Alger, Jr. The second was the boy inventor who strode onto the literary scene in such books as Alvah Milton Kerr's *Two Young Inventors* (1904) and H. L. Sayler's *The Airship Boys or, The Quest of the Aztec Treasure* (1909) and *The Airship Boys Adrift or, Saved by an Aeroplane* (1909). Taking a page from whiz-kid serial fiction, one newspaper headline called out: "Fulton, Boy Inventor, Began As Artist, Refused Reward from English for Suppressing Torpedo Device." Fulton fit the modes of the self-made American who pulled himself up by his bootstraps and the mechanically minded genius whose devices could be harnessed for the good of humankind.[8]

THE FULTON HOMESTEAD WASHINGTON COUNTY PA.

Postcard of Fulton's childhood home

Fulton was born into an impoverished family in Lancaster, Pennsylvania. When he was six years old, difficulties deepened with the death of his father. As a teenager, Fulton was apprenticed to a silversmith in Philadelphia. After a few years, he bought out his contract and supported himself by creating miniature portraits on ivory. In search of greater opportunity, he left the United States in 1787, spending the next nineteen years in England and France. Initially he devoted himself to art, studying at the Royal Academy and later with the American expatriate Benjamin West. During his mid-twenties, Fulton set aside painting as a profession to pursue scientific projects. His foray into engineering and mechanics included the design of lockless canals and improvements made to devices ranging from a rope-making machine to a torpedo-launching submarine. He even sailed a steam-powered boat on the Seine. Fulton's concepts extended beyond pure mechanics to plumb an invention's economic, political, and social implications. His time spent in Europe, punctuated by a few successes, was mostly colored by disappointment. His pronouncements on the value of his experiments fell largely on deaf ears. In Europe, and later in the United States, Fulton sought the support of rich patrons and of governments to underwrite his research and development projects. In 1806, he traveled to New York and there enjoyed his greatest triumph.[9]

The *Clermont* on the Hudson

Illustrator William J. Aylward's c.1909 watercolor captured the excitement of Fulton's 1807 voyage.

While still in France, Fulton had met Chancellor Robert Livingston of New York, a powerful and wealthy man also fascinated by steam-powered vessels. They formed a partnership called the North River Steamship Company—North River being an alternate name for the Hudson—and worked together to launch the first commercially viable steam service in the world. To much pre-event fanfare, Fulton's *North River* steamship, later referred to as the *Clermont*, began its maiden voyage on August 17, 1807. Its journey between Manhattan and Albany took a little more than thirty hours, excluding stops. The ship's return trip, with two paying passengers on board, was completed on August 19. Almost immediately, the company established a regular schedule of voyages on the Hudson, thus laying taunts of "Fulton's Folly" to rest. Initially, the financial success of this venture was assured by a patent for the steamship awarded to Fulton in 1809 coupled with a monopoly Livingston held for steam travel on the Hudson granted to him by New York State.[10]

The ship's success signaled a mastery of tides and winds that would transform the way people and goods traveled, but it did not mark the end of Fulton's struggles. In an attempt to control both the technology and its distribution, Fulton fought off competitors on the water and in court while working to expand his steamboat empire. This entrepreneurial approach would be familiar to turn-of-the-century New Yorkers. So, too, was the battle between competing technologies for dominance of the market—witness the war between Thomas Edison and George Westinghouse over the adoption of direct versus long distance electric current that raged at the turn of the twentieth century.

Fulton was at times an uneasy fit with the ideal all-American hero, due not only to early-twentieth-century assumptions about how inventors worked, but also to his questionable business practices and complex personality. Popular writers and commercial artists often portrayed Fulton as a mechanic to whom novel ideas came like sparks of genius, a stereotypic Yankee tinkerer, but his creative process actually unfolded in a much

THE CHILDREN OF HIS BRAIN

different way. He built on the ideas and the accomplishments of others, even though he was not always forthcoming in admitting these debts. For example, even though he applied for and was granted a patent, Fulton had not invented the steamboat, but rather built on the experiments of John Fitch, James Rumsey, and others, a fact that was sometimes glossed over during the Celebration. During the 1810s, to bolster his patent, Fulton tried to enlist the Earl of Stanhope, a fellow inventor in England, to verify

Harper's Weekly, **September 25, 1909**

A modern steamship, the "brain-child" of Fulton, pays homage by focusing its searchlight on his ghost.

Postcard of Fulton in his studio

that Fulton had discussed novel ideas about steamboat technology during the early 1790s. When Stanhope did not reply, Fulton faked a document that he submitted to both the New York and New Jersey Legislatures, swearing that it had been penned by Stanhope in 1793. In New Jersey, examination of the watermark revealed the date "1796" and that the paper had been manufactured in the United States, thus calling into question Fulton's honesty. During the Celebration, another aspect of his persona was either overlooked or unknown. Fulton had pursued unconventional personal relationships that would have negated his status as a role model for youth had they been revealed in 1909.[11]

During his lifetime, Fulton's dealings with highly destructive weapons were also viewed as morally questionable. Many military and political leaders considered Fulton's torpedo, and his favored delivery system the submarine, dishonorable. They took issue with the near invisibility of such an attack and with the torpedo's explosive power. They were horrified when a test ship struck by one of Fulton's torpedoes sunk a mere twenty seconds after impact, thus demonstrating that sailors on board had little chance of escape. In addition, Americans would come to learn that Fulton had not shown allegiance to the fledgling United States in the development of his weapon. Initially, Fulton had played England and France off each other to gain financial support, not approaching his own country until much later. In the hands of the English in particular, who had not yet settled their score with the United States, Fulton's weapons would have posed a threat to American navy vessels and trading ships. Claiming his weapon was actually a deterrent to war, as encapsulated in his most famous quote "the liberty of the seas will be the happiness of the earth," Fulton possessed a blinding idealism coupled with intense self-interest.[12]

Postcard

An episode that occurred early in the planning phase of the Celebration revealed the complications that could arise with Fulton. In an effort to focus on the year 1809, the Celebration organizers first considered highlighting the one-hundredth anniversary of Fulton's receiving the patent that affirmed his company's sole right to operate steamboats on the Hudson. An editorial in *The New York Times* noted the irony of commemorating an event tied to protectionism when American courts were currently dismantling transportation and industrial monopolies. Organizers reevaluated the idea of spotlighting a restriction of commerce during

The torpedo in action

Fulton demonstrated the torpedo's power on an empty ship in New York Harbor on July 20, 1807.
This illustration of the event appeared in the Lackawanna Railroad's Celebration booklet.

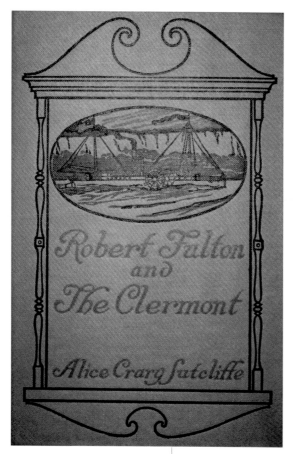

Cover of Robert Fulton biography (1909)

an era of trust-busting. Even though it was not neat from a mathematical perspective, they came to embrace 1807, rather than 1809, as the year to cheer.[13]

Although some looked at Fulton askance, others with surprisingly divergent agendas adopted him gladly. There were those who admired him as a successful entrepreneur. His experiments with seafaring weaponry also sparked pride in certain arenas at a time when the United States' interest in naval power was intense. At a Christian Socialist League of America meeting held at Carnegie Hall during the Celebration, Reverend C. S. Bullock, who had posed for a likeness of the famous inventor, announced to the crowd that Fulton would not have approved of the capitalist, unchristian system currently dominating the United States. Fulton biographer and descendant Alice Crary Sutcliffe declared that Fulton was essentially a pacifist who made overtures to peace through art, literature, and science. *The Irish-American* claimed Fulton as one of the Emerald Isle's own, even though his lineage was Scotch-Irish Protestant, not Catholic, a fact never mentioned in the article. It cast Fulton as a United Ireland freedom fighter, working in collusion with Irishmen in France and offering to take his weapons of war to Ireland to blow up English ships. According to the article, the expedition was so often postponed that he ran out of time and had to get back to the States to work on the steamboat.[14]

There were plenty of inconsistencies to knock Hudson and Fulton off their pedestals, but the two heroes survived intact, their portraits plastered everywhere and their deeds the subject of art, lectures, sermons, essays, debates, school plays, and exhibitions.[15] In his welcome speech at the official reception for foreign guests, Mayor George McClellan admitted:

It may be possible that Hudson was not the first European to see New York Harbor and that Fulton was not the first to utilize the steam engine in navigation. Yet for all practical purposes, Hudson did discover the river which bears his name, and Fulton was the first to make steam navigation a commercial success. And so, to Hudson we owe the possibility of the existence of our City, and to Fulton we owe the possibility of her prosperity.[16]

Even if Celebration organizers had to flesh out one of their leading men and tidy up the other, their contemporaries were anxious to receive Hudson and Fulton as heroes. In a scenario familiar today, Americans then were grappling with hard economic times, political corruption, social and technological transformation, and a growing immigrant population. Their worries coalesced around the newcomers and how they would be integrated into America's political, economic, and social fabric. At the time, it was widely and sensationally reported that the

birth rate among native-born Americans was declining compared to that of immigrants. (While there was some drop in the birth rate among middle- and upper-class Americans, due in part to the more widespread adoption of birth control, the statistical significance of the trend is now doubted by historians.) Even Theodore Roosevelt took up the cause, warning the National Congress of Mothers and anyone else who would listen that Anglo-Saxons were facing race extinction. This newsflash sparked fear among some Americans that immigrants would overtake the city and the country and threaten the American way of life.[17]

Part of the social critics' solution was to encourage young men and boys to adopt a strong moral code and to pursue strenuous outdoor activities as a way to become, and remain, virile. The rhetoric Governor Hughes used in one Celebration speech, urging boys "to preserve your manhood," was typical of this ethos. Emulating heroes like Henry Hudson and Robert Fulton could help American boys lead model lives. The Sons of Daniel Boone, a precursor to the Boy Scouts of America, recognized that the Hudson-Fulton Celebration offered a "high tide of hero worship." In the eyes of nativists, men like Hudson and Fulton were made of the right stuff, and they represented the "right" cultural origins.[18]

The 1909 Celebration inducted Henry Hudson and Robert Fulton into a proverbial "hall of heroes" in the regional psyche. They, in turn, offered New Yorkers an uplifting, all-American message: believe in your dream and work hard to make it a reality. In this dynamic duo, Hudson the brave explorer represented the "heart" and Fulton the skillful engineer symbolized the "head." Together, they could inspire a city, a state, and a nation. ❖

Advertising postcard featuring the Celebration's heroes

Holland-America Line postcard
Hudson is depicted as a handsome and swashbuckling adventurer.

History Parade at Columbus Circle

Parades & Politics

"The historical parade will exceed in magnificence and artistic quality anything of the kind hitherto attempted in this or any other city in the world."

New York Herald, September 21, 1909

Celebration organizers poured their dreams into two themed processions. The History of New York Parade took place on September 28, the fourth day of the Celebration. Four days later, the Carnival Parade served as Manhattan's concluding event. Recognizing that the New York experience was dominated by life in the street, civic leaders were convinced that parades could engage and educate the public. They observed how labor, socialist, anarchist, and ethnic groups used parades to attract support, instill pride, and affirm community. They could not imagine a more efficient way to share their pro-Establishment message with the same audience. These progressives envisioned the companion parades as a powerful vehicle for instructing the masses while also offering a properly modest portion of fun. Their experiment enjoyed limited success, the victim of naïveté on their part, some ill-conceived planning, and unexpected external events. In the end, the New York audience gave them a bit of a Bronx cheer.

The History of New York Parade was conceived as one of two premier events along with the opening-day flotilla of ships in New York Harbor. This "3 miles of history," with its fifty floats each costing approximately $600, was the most expensive component of the Celebration.[1] The official name of the History Parade, "the Great Historical Pageant," made clear its inspiration and organizers' lofty ambitions. In 1909, mounting a pageant was an expected part of any historical commemoration. Typically, this theatrical saga was written and performed by local citizens to mark an important anniversary and to bolster community pride. It chronicled a path of tribulations and triumphs resulting in freedom and prosperity for present-day residents. In American pageants, this good fortune was unabashedly credited to the arrival of European settlers with their high-minded values and burning work ethic. The History Parade echoed

Print of New York parade celebrating the Constitution

In 1788, when New York's ratification of the United States Constitution appeared imminent, tradespeople mounted a procession. The parade in lower Manhattan included a "federal ship of state" called the Hamilton.

the pageant's customary proud and upbeat story line.

While organizers embraced the general idea of a pageant, they rejected some of its conventions. They did not want to stage a pageant in a theater with limited seating and an admission fee. Their vision was expansive. They wanted millions of spectators to see the event for free. "This is not a rich man's show" was the Celebration's guiding mantra. Organizers wanted a "land pageant"—in other words, a parade. Scenes drawn from New York's past would be reenacted on horse-drawn flatbed trucks and pulled through city streets. The History Parade's companion event, the Carnival Parade, would be mounted in a similar manner.[2]

Celebration organizers took their cue from New York's vibrant tradition of commemorative parades and political street theater. Since the colonial period, members of trade, fraternal, and military organizations on foot and on float had honored all kinds of causes and events including the ratification of the Constitution and the conclusion of the Mexican and Spanish-American Wars. Some of the earliest parades, like the anti-Catholic Guy Fawkes Day and the pro-Irish St. Patrick's Day, were affirmations of cultural and religious allegiance. During the nineteenth century, immigrant groups continued to demonstrate their ethnic pride by marching. Celebration organizers grafted onto this tradition, hoping that by recognizing some of the diverse cultures that had contributed to New York in earlier times they could encourage the assimilation of more recent arrivals. They stated that, aside from illustrating history, their main objective in mounting the History Parade was to unite the various ethnic groups in the state.[3]

While ethnic groups had marched to express self-respect and solidarity over the years, political parties had also mounted processions as a way to drum up interest. At the turn of the twentieth century, the tradition of street rallies became all the more interesting because the public's faith in American politics was at a low point. The prevalence of political graft and violent repression of labor strikes led many Americans to conclude that the relatively unchecked power enjoyed by unscrupulous tycoons and the government officials they bribed to do their bidding imperiled fair representation for the common person. Some voters put their faith in Progressive Party politics of the sort championed by Theodore Roosevelt and Charles Evans Hughes, while the most disaffected were often attracted to socialist and anarchist movements. In the days before collective bargaining and protected workers' rights, these parties found a particularly receptive audience among members of the working class, including recent immigrants, many of whom felt helpless and disenfranchised. These alternative political parties were particularly effective in using street rallies to garner support.

As New York's civic leaders grew more worried about the popularity of these activists whom they considered provocateurs, they decided to launch their own street rally. To promote their vision of America among newcomers, organizers harkened back to the development of representational government in both New York and the United States, the securing of basic constitutional rights for individuals, and the sacrifices made to protect these rights during the colonial and early national periods.

Organizers, however, failed to include the essential ingredient in any successful parade: public input. They did not involve ordinary people in planning and production. Applying a corporate production model to this community happening, the businessmen on the parades committee decided who would design, construct, and accompany the floats per their specifications to realize their agenda. It was a one-way street. To express their ideology, they sought a uniform, traditional look for the floats. Much to the dismay of critics, they rejected artistic innovation and meaningful community participation. As one critic put it,

Postcard of float representing colonial New York's charter of liberties

FLOAT — TITLE CAR: COLONIAL PERIOD

FLOAT — TITLE CAR: UNITED STATES AND MODERN PERIOD

Postcards of floats introducing two of the History Parade's divisions

the Celebration in general, and the History Parade in particular, "was for the people, but not of them."[4]

The process of parade planning began with the hiring of a Mardi Gras veteran, Bror Wikstrom. A long-time resident of New Orleans, he created watercolor renderings which were vetted for accuracy by the historical committee. Wikstrom's unexpected death five months before the Celebration threw a jolt into parade plans. Although he died the proper artist's death—he was working at his easel—he had only completed about half of the float designs for the two parades. Other artists jumped in to create the remaining forty designs. The watercolors of individual floats were not just working drawings, but were printed as postcards and featured as illustrations in Celebration publications.[5]

As construction began, the process was covered with fanfare in New York newspapers. Reporters described how a team of 160 carpenters, sculptors, and painters created the floats in a Bronx workshop. Using a flatbed wagon as a chassis, laborers built the base of each float out of timber and chicken wire and then coated it with stucco or papier-mâché. For figures and props, workers created papier-mâché casts.[6] The design challenge was to construct a large piece of sculpture that was light in weight yet strong enough to be ridden upon and shipped to other destinations after a maiden voyage in Manhattan. The choice of papier-mâché would prove to be a mistake.

In keeping with the progressive theme intrinsic to historical pageants, the History of New York Parade was designed to illustrate the advancement and refinement of civilization. It was meant to be a literal march of and through Time.

Each of its four divisions would showcase an era in Empire State history: Native American life prior to European contact; Dutch exploration and political control of New Netherland from 1609 to 1664; English domination of the colony from 1664 to 1783; and New York after the Revolutionary War. Celebration organizers envisioned that the floats, or "moving tableaux," would provide a more exciting form of civics education than that offered solely through "books and pictures." They would be both spectacular and memorable.[7]

The organizers kept the goal of promoting allegiance to the United States front and center as they determined which events and episodes to depict. Floats fell into several categories: the growth of democracy and representative government, the establishment of municipal services, strides made in technology, and contributions made by different ethnic groups.

Many floats explored political history. Parade spectators saw scenes of Hiawatha uniting the Five Nations into the League of the Iroquois and of the election of the First Sachem of the Iroquois, Ato-tar-ho. These floats referenced the widely held belief that the founding fathers had crafted the federal system of government based on the Iroquois Confederacy.[8] Another float highlighted John Peter Zenger's landmark legal case arguing freedom of the press in 1735. Revolutionary War–related floats included the destruction of the statue of King George III on Bowling Green, the publication of the State Constitution in Kingston in 1777, and the execution of Nathan Hale "who had only one life to give for his country." George Washington taking the presidential oath of office at Federal Hall in Manhattan and the Statue of Liberty standing in New York Harbor represented the post-Revolutionary period. The commentary in the historical pageant booklet pointed out the civics lesson offered by each float.

Civic leaders in this burgeoning Metropolis were also eager to underscore advancements made in the city's public services. While there were obvious accomplishments to recognize, the choice of this theme may have also been prompted by the widespread belief that quasi-public businesses like the IRT were gouging the citizens of New York, a sentiment that William Randolph Hearst had exploited in his near-successful run for mayor in 1905. One float depicted colonists playing ninepins on Bowling Green, the earliest public park in the city, while

Postcards of floats depicting colonial and Revolutionary War scenes

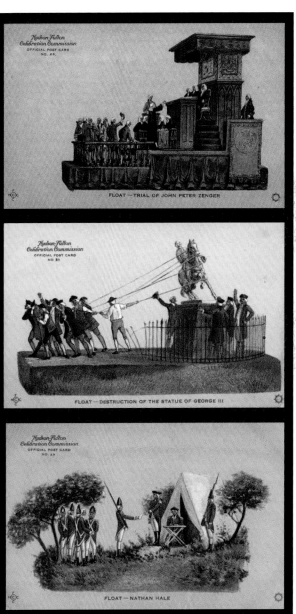

FLOAT — INTRODUCTION OF CROTON WATER

another showed old-time firemen working a hand-pumped fire engine, suggesting advancements in home and business protection. The piping of clean water to the city via the Croton Aqueduct in 1842, accompanied by a bevy of beauties portraying water nymphs, was similarly enshrined. Fulton's commercial ferry connecting Jersey City to lower Manhattan and the Broadway Sleigh, a sort of bus on runners that ran during the winter, represented achievements in mass transit. Governor DeWitt Clinton's opening of the State-sponsored Erie Canal, an important piece of infrastructure linking midwestern grain fields to New York in 1825, also appeared in float form. The official commentary noted that, thanks to the commercial explosion resulting from the canal, New York grew by leaps and bounds and achieved the status of a Metropolis.[9]

FLOAT — OLD BROADWAY SLEIGH

Postcards of floats representing New York City and State public improvements

Some floats celebrated technological innovation. This "nuts and bolts" approach to charting history ran as a thread throughout the parade. To introduce the

FLOAT — ERIE CANAL BOAT

topic of how far New Yorkers had progressed, the lead float contained two "old and new" comparisons: the wigwam and the skyscraper, the canoe and the battleship. To establish a starting point in their survey, float designers showed native people pursuing traditional crafts—fashioning tools of stone, constructing birch bark canoes, and embroidering moccasins—while colonial-era floats featured the more advanced spinning wheel and long-barreled flintlock.

Reflective of the cultural plurality of colonial New York, and as a signal to the diverse audience organizers hoped to reach, the History Parade recognized contributions made by various ethnicities. While falling far short of twenty-first-century standards for cultural sensitivity and inclusion, the organizers made some effort. In keeping with the concept of the parade, the historical personages depicted were primarily Native American, Dutch, English, and American. There were also four French-related floats, including ones dedicated to Governor Jacob Leisler's deeding his land in New Rochelle to the Huguenots and the Marquis de Lafayette's return tour of the United States in 1824–1825. Italy was represented by a single float. It depicted the residence of the freedom fighter Giuseppe Garibaldi, who lived on Staten Island while in exile during the 1850s. To escort the floats, organizers extended invitations to fraternal organizations composed of "citizens of African, Bohemian, Danish, Dutch, English, French, German, Hungarian, Irish, Italian, Norwegian, Polish, Scotch, Swedish, and Syrian descent."[10] At the end of the History of New York Parade, the final float, called "Father Knickerbocker Receiving," featured a gigantic patriarchal

Postcard of float introducing the History Parade

Above and left: **Postcards of floats highlighting tools and technology**

FLOAT — COLONIAL HOME

figure welcoming immigrants from many lands to New York.

While some ethnic groups may have yearned for more attention in the Celebration's festivities, the Iroquois probably wanted less. Short on specifics and long on stereotype, the Indian-themed floats focused on daily life as shaped by the changing seasons. Celebration organizers were especially proud that they had gone to the trouble to engage actual Iroquois people to participate when it would have been far easier to use non-Indian reenactors. "Secured from the Indian reservations for the Commission by Mr. F. E. Moore and . . . dressed in their picturesque native costumes,"[11] some seventy men, women, and children performed dances amidst papier-mâché confections of Plains Indian teepees and giant war bonnets. If the cultural inaccuracies weren't insult enough, marching members of Tammany Hall dressed as Indians accompanied the native performers. Commentators remarked that seeing the Iroquois participants caused excitement, particularly among foreign dignitaries.

Perhaps to assure some brighter moments, organizers included a few floats with guaranteed popular appeal. The "Fate of Hudson" float, depicting the explorer's abandonment by his mutinous crew in Canada's James Bay, featured icebergs and polar bears, imagery spectators would immediately associate with Peary and Cook's fight over the North Pole. For all their claims of historical accu-

Iroquois at a Celebration reception held at Columbia University

Popular Wild West shows such as Buffalo Bill Cody's set the tone for Native American participation and performance.

racy, organizers spiffed up the "Saint Nicholas" float by substituting the far cheerier, New York-born Santa Claus with his sleigh, reindeer, and bundle of toys for the more somber and less generous Old World bishop. In addition, Washington Irving's popular fictional stories "Rip Van Winkle" and "The Legend of Sleepy Hollow," couched as tales typical of the colonial period, appeared as floats.[12]

New York newspapers trumpeted the History Parade for weeks and months prior.[13] Their bravura turned embarrassing the day of the event. The History Parade did not live up to the expectations of discerning organizers and spectators. Bad luck played a hand, while other problems resulted from the corporate mode of parade production and execution coupled with the ambitious, high-minded, but ultimately unrealistic goals of the elites who organized the parade.

Some viewers complained that the floats lacked artistry and were poorly constructed. "It needed much faith and great good nature not to laugh at the painted canvas-rocks and blazing fires of papier-mâché amidst which this nation

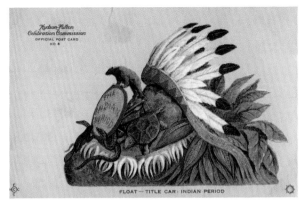

FLOAT — TITLE CAR: INDIAN PERIOD

FLOAT — FATE OF HENRY HUDSON

Postcard of float introducing the Indian period division

Postcard of float representing the fate of Hudson

Saint Nicholas float on Central Park West

seems to have worked out its earliest destinies" according to one reporter. He went on to say that perhaps "a gilded paper naiad pouring a stream of cheese-cloth out of a paper cornucopia might appeal" for a nighttime, rather than a day-time, parade. *The Craftsman* magazine noted that the "gaudy, shaky floats" were made all the more abhorrent because no architects or artists from New York had been invited to help design them. Another critic urged that competent artists, rather than "the practical man," take charge the next time New York constructed parade floats.[14]

Clearly sore over the criticism, the parade committee later defended itself, claiming the floats:

were not intended to be beaux arts productions nor was it expected that the modeling and coloring would be according to fine arts standards. They were, however, designed and constructed by the most expert artisans available in this kind of pageant work and no pains were spared to have the workmanship conform to the best standard of this class of handicraft.[15]

Upon reflection, the organizers thought that the floats were too large. Their monumental scale, conceived with the backdrop of city buildings in mind, con-tributed to their instability and prevented some floats from reaching parade locations outside of Manhattan.[16]

Another target of criticism was the prominent role of political clubs and civil service workers in the parade. Although the organizers made much of the fact that the people riding on, or escorting, the floats were descendants of the historical figures portrayed, or had some meaningful connection to them, critics noted that many participants did not look engaged, but rather were "uninter-ested, unenthusiastic individuals who were paid to dress up in clothes which made them self-conscious and awkward." Incongruous appearances included a surprising number of Revolutionary War heroes who smoked cigarettes and males clearly filling some female roles—including a gentleman with very visible beard stubble playing Queen Anne and a colonial "woman" in a Dutch doorway smoking a cigar. Nowhere was this more pointed than with the Indian floats which were accompanied by members of the Order of Red Men and Tammany Hall, some of whom wore buckskin and "red face." Not only were they not Native American, but they symbolized political corruption. The inclusion of Sheriff Foley, Battery Dan Finn, and their compatriots seemed all the more ironic because they marched at the start of the parade, immediately undermining the organizers' claim that they would not allow graft to touch the Celebration.[17]

The use of papier-mâché, a water-soluble material, also caused grief. A deluge of rain during the hours leading up to the History Parade posed a huge threat. Fearing the parade would literally melt away, organizers delayed its start. According to the official story, the clouds broke before they had to cancel the parade outright, but the delay did not give workers time to put the floats in proper order. A jumble of floats representing different parade divisions and time periods ensued. One article noted that Clio, the goddess of history, "got her dates mixed" as President George Washington took his oath of office seven blocks before Henry Hudson discovered the Hudson River. The chronological sequencing so integral to illustrating the progressive nature of history was lost. Cynics laughed at the absurdities, while less critical spectators looked on in confusion. In their own defense, desperate organizers stated that spectators had printed programs at their disposal to help them put floats in proper order in their own minds, so this mix-up was not a big problem.[18]

For some in the audience, the lack of chronological order was not an issue. One observer noted the deep interest of school-aged children, who, recognizing scenes from their history books, pointed them out to their elders. For twelve-

Croton Aqueduct float
Floats such as this one, with its lavish use of cheesecloth and paper, were criticized for their garish appearance and shoddy fabrication.

History Parade lining up at 110th Street and Central Park West

Organizers blamed bad weather for the chaos that marked the parade's formation.

year-old Marie Greenfield, a recent arrival to Manhattan from Danzig in present-day Poland, the History Parade offered high entertainment at a time when her family had no extra money for amusements. As she recalled the parade floats later in life, "much of it we didn't understand, but what wonderful bits of Americana these were for the newcomers around the turn of the century."[19]

Even if the History Parade had gone off as planned, the organizers' expectations were unrealistic. Relying on commentary in a souvenir booklet was foolhardy. Most of the spectators had not purchased the booklet and, even if they had, many in the crowd could not read English fluently. How could they ascertain the subject matter of each float, much less comprehend how all fifty floats came together to illustrate the progressive nature of New York history? All this said, as evidenced by the size of the crowd—which was estimated to be one million—the superlative newspaper headlines, and the hasty jottings on the backs of postcards, viewers in general found the History Parade exciting.[20]

Organizers devised the Carnival Parade as a complement to the History Parade. Whereas the History Parade highlighted a shared past, the Carnival Parade focused on a shared culture. The Carnival Parade drew directly on the custom of nocturnal party-parades with costumes, music, and song mounted in Cologne, Paris, New Orleans, and other cities to mark the end of winter and the start of Lent. By the mid-nineteenth century, these urban celebrations had lost some of their freeness and bacchanalian flavor as groups formally organized festivities that made allusion to classical music, theater, and fine art. Celebration organizers viewed an appreciation of the "intellectual culture from the Old World" among the general population as an indicator of civilization's progress. The Carnival Parade was mounted on the last evening of Manhattan's festivities.[21]

Unlike the History Parade, which was designed to focus on one theme and to present it in chronological order, the Carnival Parade mined various subjects—art, ancient history, mythology, literature, and northern European culture—and presented all as a merry potpourri. In this assortment of floats, "Medusa" rubbed shoulders with "The Elves of Spring," while "Father Rhine" found himself parading with "Egyptian Art, Music, and Literature." Floats at the beginning and end of the parade offered a serious message. The lead float, a tribute to the arts, was followed by one devoted to Mars, the god of war, and minor goddesses who

Carnival Parade booklet

Float depicting Washington's farewell to his officers at Fraunces Tavern in lower Manhattan

represented "the evils which attend war."[22] This pairing of art and war suggests anxiety about the bellicosity that marked the international situation in 1909 and the thought that the arts might be a fruitful way of bringing people together. The Carnival Parade's final float, showing Uncle Sam formally greeting foreign dignitaries in a diplomatic court setting, echoed this hope.

While the Carnival Parade's subject matter was wide-ranging overall, nearly half of the floats referenced Northern European music, folklore, and history. The long list of German, Swiss, and Austrian-related floats included "The Crowning of Beethoven," "Lohengrin," "William Tell," "Siegfried," "Heidelberg," "Bavaria," "The God of the Alps," and "Andreas Hoffer, a Real Hero of the Tyrol." Austrian, Swiss, and German singing and fraternal societies accompanied the fifty floats.[23] This broadly Germanic emphasis was meant to counterbalance the

Postcards of Carnival Parade floats

FLOAT — GERMANIA

FLOAT — FROST KING

FLOAT — LOHENGRIN

FLOAT — GNOMES

A sampling of floats with Germanic themes

accent on the Dutch and English in the History Parade. Through the Carnival Parade, Celebration organizers reached out to Germans and German Americans who made up a sizeable percentage of New York's population in 1909, but who had not played a significant role in the development of early New York.

By having the singing societies march alongside the floats, Celebration planners mimicked community traditions that were familiar to their audience. As in their homeland, Germans in America joined social clubs based on common interests, occupations, politics, or origins. Among these clubs, musical associations were particularly popular. Beginning in the mid-nineteenth century, an era of large-scale German emigration to the United States, choral groups gathered in cities for competitive "sing-offs" called *Sängerfests*. These battles of the choirs were a source of pleasure and camaraderie for participants, while also helping to assure Americans that Germanic culture was refined. Singing societies moved beyond the confines of concert halls to march in parades alongside lodges, military groups, and occupational organizations. In one highly memorable event, singing society members, along with tens of thousands of other German Americans, paraded in Manhattan to mark the end of the Franco-Prussian War and the formation of the German Empire in 1871.[24]

The Carnival Parade's emphasis on "the Teutonic and Alpine races" to the exclusion of other ethnic groups met with mixed approval. One critic praised the spectacle of 15,000 German, Austrian, and Swiss float escorts carrying sticks of red, white, and green fire and the "buxom maidens and athletic youths" who portrayed characters from famous German operas. Another was puzzled as to why there were so many German floats. In positioning Germanic culture as the main theme—to the exclusion of Italian, Irish, Jewish, African, and central European culture—organizers tacitly pointed toward a "good" ethnic group they considered model.[25]

Like the History Parade, the Carnival Parade was also hampered by events beyond the control of the organizers. A few days before the start of the Celebration, the Police Commissioner banned masks, costumes, confetti, and ticklers. He feared the repeat of an incident that had taken place a few days before at a Mardi Gras-themed parade at Coney Island where a band of roughs had run and pushed their way through dense crowds assaulting people. With the whole world watching, New Yorkers were going to have to behave, even if it meant a lack of spontaneous gaiety. A carnival without any party in the streets was a bit of a bust, and especially confusing to young people. Gustav Stickley put his finger on the problem when he noted that this approach to organizing parades failed because it cast the people on the streets as impassive observers rather than as engaged merrymakers. Applying a bureaucratic model to parade- and carnival-making was not successful. The reformers' message to "have fun, but not too much of it" ran counter to the long-lived parade and carnival traditions of mocking authority, assuming different identities, and behaving in an excessive manner.[26]

When all was said and done, the History and Carnival Parades were amusing diversions. Crowds watched from grandstands, door stoops, sidewalks, and soapboxes. An irreverent spirit crept in here and there. Wiseacres in the crowd yelled out witticisms. Men dressed up as women. Bands, expected to play an all-Sousa march repertoire, broke into ragtime tunes and current hits like Irving Berlin's "My Wife's Gone to the Country, Hurrah, Hurrah" with its refrain "I love my wife, but oh you kid!"[27]

While the messages intended may have been ambiguous to, or just plain ignored by, the viewers, the content and structure of these street pageants nevertheless reflected the goals of Celebration organizers. They mounted the History Parade in hopes of making New York's past lively, accessible, and

Sheet music for *Hudson-Fulton March* and *My Wife's Gone to the Country*

To the distress of some and the delight of many, bands in the parades often played popular tunes instead of traditional marches.

understandable to a broad audience. The line of floats representing historical themes and events was supposed to show how civilization had progressed upward in New York. The Carnival Parade was envisioned as a tribute to high culture, which the committee of elites determined was Germanic culture. Organizers promulgated a message they considered critical to the nation's political stability. The History and Carnival Parades, each in its own way, were meant to convince spectators that, while New Yorkers might come from different ethnic backgrounds, they shared a common history and culture and owed ultimate allegiance to the United States. ❖

"First Stars and Stripes" division

This tribute was part of the children's festival at the New York Botanical Garden.

THE
Littlest Knickerbockers
on Parade

"But they are busy, every man Jack and girl Jill. And teachers and mothers are busy. Saturday, October 2, will see a page of history—yes, two pages—come to life for the boys and girls of 1909. Think of the numbers of citizens-to-be, the Americans of tomorrow, who are saluting the flag in broken speech and who will play their part in a replica of the drama whose first presentation found their ancestors far from the scene of action. . . . But when they finish they will be better Americans, with a keener appreciation of what the growth of a nation means."

The Evening Post, September 25, 1909

Throughout the two-week history fair, civic leaders spoke passionately about the positive effect the Celebration could have on the younger generation, the hope of the future. While girls and boys participated in many events up and down the Hudson, organizers earmarked two days' worth of festivities in New York City where students served as both the actors and the audience. These were Education Day on September 29 and Children's Day on October 2. Within the Hudson-Fulton Celebration program structure, children were allowed the greatest leeway in fashioning their own historical tributes and expressing their ethnic pride. While some of their programs might resemble child's play, this was American citizenship education first and foremost.

Education Day, also called Commemoration Day, took place in classrooms and auditoriums. Celebration officials believed that the public schools would do more than any other agency "to put red blood and a true spirit into the coming celebration. . . . Let the pupils read much of the history which makes the Empire State so great. Let them write upon it. Let the exercises upon the 29th of September be public and popular." They rightly recognized that the New York public school system was an effective acculturator of recent arrivals, and this was no mean feat. In 1909, *The New York Times* reported that Gotham schools had the highest number of foreign-born children of

Celebration songbook

any city in the world. In order to make the most of this special opportunity, Celebration advisors authored instructional pamphlets to help guide teachers and parents in choosing appropriate activities and historical subject matter for both Education Day and Children's Day exercises.[1]

On Education Day, students performed in plays and formed living tableaux, debated historical topics, read aloud essays they had written in hopes of winning a medal, and joined in songs and salutes to flag and country. They attended lectures, some of which were illustrated by lantern slides. They also fashioned arts and crafts.[2] Even before the academic year had started, handiwork made by youth in summer camps offered a preview of the cascade of tributes that students would produce in their school art classes come September. At the children's festival headquarters in Brooklyn in early August:

The committee room is already well stocked with tiny Clermonts, whittled out of wood, finished with modeling clay and decorated with sails. There are Indian birch bark canoes, Indian costumes of such gaudiness that it would have startled the eyes even of the aborigines. There are wooden shoes, hand carved; windmills and sets of old-fashioned furniture. As yet, of course, only the children that come to vacation schools and playgrounds or attend settlement clubs have had their hand at the making, but when all the school children are set to work there is no doubt that thousands of tomahawks, snowshoes, Dutch and Indian costumes will be ready, the work of the boys and girls themselves.[3]

One of several instructional booklets issued for the Celebration

Collage showing kitties preparing for the Celebration

Kittens are reading history, writing essays, and knitting socks to be worn when parading.

We're working for the "Hudson-Fulton,"
You see we're patriotic quite,
Altho' we're only little kittens
We know our duty and what's right.

One reads aloud the history
That all about New York does tell,
'Bout Hudson and the Indian people
And Fulton's boat that sailed so well.

Another's writ a composition.
You see we're educated high.
What, you can't read it? well, you know
'Tis writ in "Palmer," that is why.

The third works harder still than these.
She's knitting socks for all our paws.
We'll want them on our tender feet,
When we parade, in the mighty cause.

Cross-stitched needlework picture of the *Clermont*

Many of Education Day's in-classroom projects were inspired by the work of the City History Club, created by New York elites in 1896 as a "kindergarten of citizenship" for foreign and native-born children. On its own—and by collaborating with Lillian Wald's Henry Street Settlement, the University Settlement, and other social settlements—the Club engaged youth through history-based arts and crafts projects, exhibitions, and field trips.[4] Experiential learning helped instill the political and cultural messages inherent in the Celebration.

On Children's Day, nearly a million youngsters citywide took to the streets and parks, parading, dancing, and starring in pageants. Its offerings were the most varied and inclusive in spirit, a reflection of local committees' active role in planning and implementation. Initially, organizers had assumed that children

Supervised play

This detail of a proposed playground for the Lower East Side appeared in Harper's Weekly, *December 28, 1895.*

Dutch girls and the Sons of Liberty

Young reenactors march to the children's festival at the New York Botanical Garden in the Bronx.

would march in Manhattan's History of New York Parade, but then realized that the littlest Knickerbockers did not possess the stamina to withstand the six-mile-long route. Organizers came up with a neighborhood-focused program as the alternative. While the Celebration's History and Carnival Parades received criticism as artificial, forced, and lacking in intentional humor, the Children's Day parades were creative, engaging, and full of fun. This was a true holiday as defined by anthropologists, where the weakest members of society are allowed to rule, where children were invited to walk on the grass in parks and to march down the center of Fifth Avenue while the police had to stand back and watch.[5]

Even though there was ample opportunity for personal expression, Children's Day festivities conformed to an overall framework. On Saturday afternoon, in forty-six districts across the city, students rallied in their schoolyards. Some were dressed in historical garb or folk dress while others wore street clothes and carried little flags. They processed to nearby parks where those in costume performed pageants, drills, and dances for the other children and adults. All were encouraged to join in patriotic salutes and songs before marching back to school. Celebration advisors insisted that divisions be identified with placards, line up in chronological order in history parades, and strive for accuracy down to the tiniest detail. These touches would help marchers and spectators appreciate the event's value as a lesson in history and citizenship.[6]

Within the prescribed format, parents and other members of the local committees had freedom to mount their own spectacles. Descriptions in newspapers conjure up images of "Busby Berkeley meets Yankee Doodle," with waves of costumed children posing, dancing, and drilling. On Staten Island's River Lake, boys in sailors' outfits manned miniature versions of the *Half Moon* and the *Clermont* while others wearing wigwam suits formed an Indian village on shore. In a similar but more interactive scene near Inwood, boys outfitted in Dutch costume sailed in a replica *Half Moon* while classmates dressed as Indians attacked them with bows and arrows. In Brooklyn's Fort Greene, children mounted a miniature parade with floats, including "Leif Ericson and the Vikings discovering North America in 1000 A.D." crafted by young Norwegians. At Battery Park, with assistance from the group Little Mother's Aid, children representing Native Americans, Dutch settlers, British redcoats, and American Revolutionary War soldiers marched to the applause of thousands. Their pageant consisted of scenes drawn from colonial history interspersed with folk dances performed by Syrian and Russian girls. The latter executed "whirling Dervish dances," while on a nearby lawn the historical characters of George and Martha Washington served tea to audience members.[7]

Many of the recitals featured folk dancing. At the Court of Honor, the official parade reviewing stand, costumed children from public and private schools,

Photograph of African-American children dressed as Indians

Nearly invisible to Celebration organizers, African Americans were, for the most part, kept at the periphery of the event, even though they had lived in New York since the early seventeenth century. Unlike other ethnic groups, during the children's festivals young African Americans did not represent their own cultural origins in dress, music, or dance.

church groups, orphanages, and settlement houses performed for Governor Charles Evans Hughes, philanthropist Mrs. Russell Sage, and Tammany boss Dan Finn. Their recital of ten dances included an Indian snake dance, a Dutch dance, and a colonial minuet.

Little girl angels contributed a peace dance. African-American girls from the Abyssinian Baptist Church performed a Japanese dance. Next, Hungarian girls in traditional dress took the floor. An instructional pamphlet explained that the folk dances of all nations, performed in succession and then in unison as one people, were an appropriate form of rejoicing. To this day, the tradition of public school children performing recitals of folk dances outdoors is alive and well in New York City.[8]

The early twentieth century's widespread appreciation of folk or traditional cultures can be linked to two nineteenth-century movements: the rise of nationalism in Europe and the arts and crafts philosophy that put high value on the

Girls in Dutch costume dancing in the Court of Honor

Weller Pottery teapot
Weller was one of several art potteries to produce Dutch-inspired ceramics at this time. It unveiled its Holland and Dresden lines, featuring windmills and Dutch peasants, between 1907 and 1909.

pre-industrial past. By 1900, scholars were documenting folkways and collecting folk artifacts. Cutting-edge educators saw the use of folk dance, especially among children, as a suitable vehicle to show ethnic pride while still fitting within the strictures of dominant American culture. In the Children's Day dance programs, some young ones represented their own cultural origins, while others were encouraged to adopt the trappings of cultures that were not their own.

Many danced and dressed in a Dutch style. At face value, these children were paying homage to New York's early history, but there was something more here. Their Dutch dance and dress also referenced the stereotype of the Dutch peasant that was particularly popular in literature and art during this era. As America at large worried about the millions of immigrants entering the nation—many of whom were poor, uneducated, and forced by finances to live a horrific existence in slums—the idealized world of the Dutch peasant offered a different view. Here quaint country people wearing colorful folk dress and wooden shoes strolled amidst windmills and tulips. These were the "good peasants"—blonde-haired, blue-eyed, healthy, clean, industrious, and non-threatening. They represented northern, rather than central or southern, Europe and thus were seen as less strange and more culturally acceptable by mainstream America. Their fairy-tale existence knew none of the social ills and harsh conditions associated with extreme urban poverty. Hans Brinker and his ilk were suitable models for all, but particularly for newcomers.[9]

Postcard of Uncle Sam arm-in-arm with Dutch woman

In 1909, parades and dance programs offered a metaphorical invitation for all children to "get in step" culturally and politically. To do so was hard work. To prepare for Children's Day, training camps were established during the summer. Instructors led children in marches and dance drills, teaching them about the "history and spirit of New York," and, according to one newspaper, encouraging them to act as "a congress of nations" by displaying loyalty to New York's symbolic figure Father Knickerbocker. At these camps, the young learned that during Children's Day exercises, as in real life, it was fine to express ethnic pride, and even to dance to one another's tunes, but ultimately Uncle Sam and Father Knickerbocker set the beat. Advisors suggested having one or both of these iconic figures march with a group of children as the perfect ending to a neighborhood parade.[10]

School children's pageant at the New York Botanical Garden

Historical characters pay homage to a figure representing America.

Pageants, performed both on Children's Day and Education Day, were plentiful and full of import. One program featured a march through time by grade, with the youngest elementary students portraying Indians and the fourth through sixth grades honoring the Dutch, English, and American periods of New York history. The seventh and eighth graders presented tributes to the Hudson River. During the finale, the figure of Father Knickerbocker called upon all nationalities to participate. Elsewhere, an allegorical play of New World and Old World interdependence told how glorious and strong Europa assisted her younger and weaker sister Columbia by sending explorers and settlers to extract her riches.[11] In a pageant authored and performed by students at Public School No. 6:

The Spirit of the Hudson summoned her daughters, the cities on her banks, and as they formed a group around her, bands of immigrants from across the ocean entered and knelt at the feet of the Spirit of New York. Each group told of the hope that had inspired their coming. The Spirit of New York, with pride in her power but humility at her shortcomings, asked what she could do to better the conditions of the newcomers. The immigrants made impassioned pleas for better tenement house conditions, cleaner streets, more playgrounds, better excise laws and a filtration plant for the city water. The Spirit of the Hudson pleaded for the purification of her waters and the preservation of her forests and scenic beauties. The Spirit of New York and the immigrants pledged themselves to strive for these things.[12]

Noble sentiments expressed through solemn oratory ruled the Celebration's pageantry, but there was the rare exception. For a production at St. Agnes School in Brooklyn, Sister M. Petra penned a comedy involving Hudson, Fulton, President Taft, and former President Roosevelt. It was a near miracle. The *New York Press* marveled that though the author had never seen the inside of a theater, her comic play "has been pronounced a brilliant skit."[13]

Sister Petra's light-hearted approach was unusual. Celebration organizers had earmarked the unification of New York's diverse population as a main goal and they targeted immigrant children as particularly critical. They believed that if children adopted the persona and dress of figures from American history, they would be more likely to identify with the values these characters represented. Using stingingly insensitive stereotypes, one reporter noted in the thrilling days

leading up to the Celebration that little "Abies and Pietros and Patsys and Wilhelms will find themselves in the guise of Fulton," and predicted that with "many a flag salute given in broken English," these impressionable youngsters would grow to be better Americans. After the event, another reporter observed "thus timid foreigners were encouraged to learn in this manner more of the traditions and history of their new country. 'The Melting Pot' of which Zangwill speaks boiled merrily."[14]

"The Melting Pot" referred to Israel Zangwill's popular play about immigrant life that had opened out of town in 1908, ran in New York in 1909, and introduced this phrase into the American lexicon. A sort of "West Side Story" but set in Queens and with a happier ending, the drama tells the story of two young Russian immigrants, one Jewish and the other Christian, who fall in love. When the young man learns that his beloved is the daughter of the tsarist officer responsible for the pogrom that drove him from his homeland, they separate. Eventually they reunite, envisioning a future free of cultural and religious prejudice. Near the play's end, the young man looks out over the Statue of Liberty and cries "there she lies, the great Melting-Pot—Listen! Can't you hear the roaring and the bubbling?" Zangwill's melting pot was a crucible, and it churned violently, in contrast to the "merry boil" of Children's Day festivities.[15]

Harper's Weekly, **February 13, 1892**

ENTERING A NEW WORLD
" See the Daystar of Liberty Rise "

The phrase came to represent a concept of assimilation more benign than the play's author intended. As commonly used in the United States, "the melting pot" referred to a large number of immigrants representing various nationalities and cultures blending together to form a fairly homogeneous society. Immigrants were invited to bring aspects of their culture to share at the table, but they had to let go of some old ways in order to become Americans. Implicit was the idea that newcomers were welcome to contribute to the stew, but the dominant flavor would remain Anglo-American. They were expected to assimilate culturally, linguistically, and politically. During the twentieth century, notions of acculturation changed, with the "tossed salad" and its distinct ingredients representing the different concept of multiculturalism by century's end.

In 1909, New York's elites knew that they could not take for granted the allegiance and complacency of laborers and their families, whose ranks included many immigrants. Historian Howard Zinn considers 1908 a watershed year, when civic leaders recognized, and actively responded to, the growing influence of the International Workers of the World, trade unions, socialists, and anarchists. In a telling newspaper story, a reporter visited a Sunday school for children run by anarchists, a loosely associated group who placed their faith in local cooperative efforts rather than national governments. In their current events discussion, students observed how the individual sailors from different countries had shown friendship to each other on land during the Hudson-Fulton Celebration and wondered why navies would want to fight at sea. The reporter concluded from such talk that "these little anarchists are being trained to believe in no authority," a fear shared by mainstream America. The battle for hearts and minds was on. Civic leaders hoped that the Celebration's instructive amusements would promote patriotic sentiments among the young and inoculate them against the lure of alternative political parties.[16]

Education Day and Children's Day programs modeled what it meant to be an American, promoting unity of ideas among the next generation of citizens. With the patriarchal characters of Father Knickerbocker and Uncle Sam setting the tone, the flurry of marching, acting, singing, dancing, writing, and art-making was designed to instill American spirit and loyalty among young ones of varying cultural origins. School officials, settlement house workers, and community volunteers directed and buoyed the children's efforts. Governor Charles Evans Hughes believed that, through the study of New York's history, "we are electrifying youth"[17]—a reference to the Celebration's exhilarating nighttime displays. He and his contemporaries prayed that their brand of civic virtue would burn on brightly long after this history fair's finale. ❖

J. P. Morgan acquiring treasures from around the world

This cartoon of the avid art collector and his "money magnet" appeared in the June 21, 1911 issue of Puck Magazine.

Jump-Starting New York's Arts & Culture

" In the Van Cortlandt House [in the Bronx] were shown Wedgwood medallion portraits and mezzotints of illustrious personages who lived prior to the Revolution; cartoons and caricatures of political events, etc. This old house with its Colonial furnishings, gave to those who came here a better idea of the surroundings in which the founders of the country lived, moved, and had their being, than could be acquired by long study of printed records. There have been nearly 300,000 visitors during the past year."

Edward Hagaman Hall, *The Hudson-Fulton Celebration 1909*

A lthough hard to imagine now, New York in 1909 was not yet a cultural capital. During the mid-twentieth century, the city secured its position as an internationally recognized arts capital, but half a century earlier that outcome was far from certain. At that time, in the arts arena, New York barely held its own against Boston and Philadelphia.[1] Parity with Berlin, Paris, or London lay in the future. Realizing that all imperial cities rested on a strong foundation of arts and culture, Celebration organizers desperately wanted to rectify this deficiency. They associated the flourishing of cultural institutions with urban ascendency and saw the Celebration as a vehicle for showcasing and strengthening the art life of this aspiring world city.

When writing about the roster of museum exhibitions in the Celebration's official report, organizers revealed the expansive scope of their ambitions:

The aim of the Commission was not confined to honoring the explorer of the Hudson River and the man who made steam navigation a permanent success; in addition to this the occasion was utilized to illustrate and emphasize the development and greatness of New York City, the Metropolis of the western hemisphere. Those who can understand the true significance of this Celebration, and who are able to forecast the future, will see the vision of a still greater and more magnificent city, worthy of being called a world Metropolis.[2]

In their attempt to buttress New York's shaky cultural profile, Commission members rejected some of the standard features associated with world's fairs.

Crystal Palace interior

London's Crystal Palace of 1851, considered the first international exposition, showcased contemporary arts and industries, thus establishing the custom of manufacturers creating elaborate arrangements of commercial wares and *tour de force* pieces in rented booths within vast exhibition halls. At their worst, commemorative expositions had become little more than glorified trade shows, disguising business boosterism within the cloak of education. During the planning process, Hudson-Fulton Celebration organizers flatly refused to host this type of display.[3] At New York's commemorative festival, exhibitions would focus on history and art, not merchandise.

Bucking convention even further, organizers decided not to create fairgrounds. Instead, they encouraged cultural institutions to mount exhibitions at their own facilities. Organizers saw multiple benefits to this strategy. With the whole city on display, residents and visitors alike would gain a greater appreciation of its riches, and put more stock in its claim as a great Metropolis. Thanks to an extensive mass transit system, people could travel to cultural institutions throughout the five boroughs with relative ease. Participating institutions could leverage the general excitement generated by the Celebration to attract more donations and visitors. The businessmen in charge also realized that by foregoing the construction of a world's fair-type campus, they could save lots of money. To justify their reliance on existing institutions, they offered an elaborate if somewhat clunky financial equation:

To apply the standard of monetary value may seem a trifle vulgar when we are treating . . . the triumphs of art in all its forms, and yet this standard merely expresses the worth of antiquities and artistic creations in a more exact way than by using superlatives of speech. A reasonable estimate of the value of the attractions which New York City offers to its visitors would be rather in excess of $2,000,000,000 than below that figure, and yet, where the great expositions of the past have cost from $10,000,000 to $20,000,000 or more for their organization, all the treasures and the beauties of New York can be displayed at an expense of only $1,000,000.[4]

The organizers used the topic of museum exhibitions as a way to express their greatest aspirations for the city. The million-dollar figure cited actually referred to the price tag for the entire Celebration, not the more modest $22,000 the Commission granted to help underwrite the program of exhibitions.[5]

Proposed exposition campus for the Hudson-Fulton Celebration at Verplanck's Point

Early in the planning, this extraordinary rendering appeared in Harper's Weekly, January 19, 1907. Organizers eventually rejected the idea of building any fairgrounds.

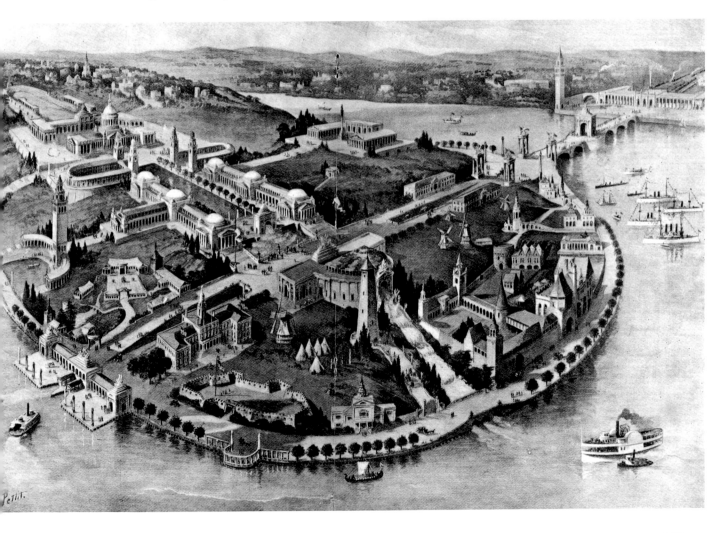

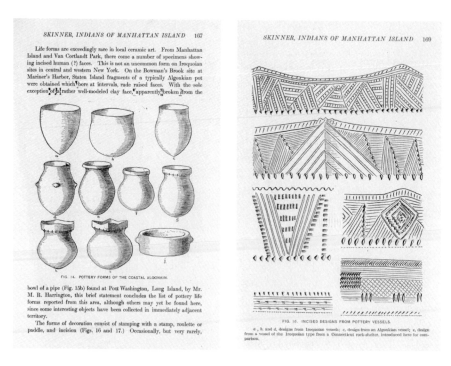

Life forms are exceedingly rare in local ceramic art. From Manhattan Island and Van Cortlandt Park, there come a number of specimens showing incised human (?) faces. This is not an uncommon form on Iroquoian sites in central and western New York. On the Bowman's Brook site at Mariner's Harbor, Staten Island fragments of a typically Algonkian pot were obtained which bore at intervals, rude raised faces. With the sole exception of a rather well-modeled clay face, apparently broken from the

FIG. 14. POTTERY FORMS OF THE COASTAL ALGONKIN.

bowl of a pipe (Fig. 15b) found at Port Washington, Long Island, by Mr. M. R. Harrington, this brief statement concludes the list of pottery life forms reported from this area, although others may yet be found here, since some interesting objects have been collected in immediately adjacent territory.

The forms of decoration consist of stamping with a stamp, roulette or paddle, and incision (Figs. 16 and 17.) Occasionally, but very rarely,

FIG. 16. INCISED DESIGNS FROM POTTERY VESSELS.

a, b, and d, designs from Iroquoian vessels; c, design from an Algonkian vessel; e, design from a vessel of the Iroquoian type from a Connecticut rock-shelter, introduced here for comparison.

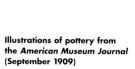

Illustrations of pottery from the *American Museum Journal* (September 1909)

This publication accompanied a popular exhibition on Native American life mounted at the American Museum of Natural History.

In all, twenty-two museums, historic houses, historical societies, clubs, libraries, parks, and zoos within the city mounted special exhibitions. Curators pursued two types of programs: those paying homage to the people, plants, and animals native to pre-contact New York and those exploring the worlds of Henry Hudson and Robert Fulton.

Appreciation of the indigenous was a relatively recent phenomenon circa 1900. This cultural value developed as a reaction to the uniformity associated with ever-growing industrialization and to the widespread introduction of non-native plants and animals. Americans and Europeans alike began to value disappearing people, cultures, animals, and plants as their existence was threatened. In a quest to honor what was distinctive about New York, anthropologists and scientists mounted a number of exhibitions. The American Museum of Natural History addressed the daily lives and material culture of the Weesquaeseeks, Reckgawawancs, and other Indians who had lived in the lower Hudson Valley prior to European contact. The newly formed New York Botanical Garden labeled specimen trees native to the Hudson Valley while the Parks Department did the same for flowers and plants. The New York Aquarium, then housed in lower Manhattan's Castle Garden, highlighted species that had been swimming in the Hudson River at the time of the *Half Moon*'s voyage. The New York Zoological Park in Central Park similarly paid tribute to mammals and birds indigenous to Manhattan.[6]

Other institutions focused on Hudson, Fulton, or the eras they represented. The National Arts Club, the Lenox Branch of the New York Public Library, the American Geographical Society, and other organizations assembled paintings, prints, maps, and manuscripts. The New-York Historical Society and the Colonial Dames of America co-sponsored an exhibition on Robert Fulton in the society's newly completed Henry Dexter Hall. The American Society of Mechanical Engineers honored their kindred spirit Fulton, displaying his artwork as well as models of early and modern steamships.[7]

Of all the exhibitions connected to the Celebration, those mounted at the Metropolitan Museum of Art caused the most excitement, had the most impact, and rate as most significant today. They symbolized the coming of age of art collecting and appreciation in the United States, as wealthy Americans began to dominate the European art market and museum curators and visitors began to value early American paintings and furnishings as art objects rather than simply as antiquarian curiosities.

Dutch art exhibition at the Metropolitan Museum in 1909

In 1909, the Metropolitan Museum was not yet the world-class institution it would become. Since its founding in 1870, the fledgling museum had displayed plaster casts of antique statuary as it struggled to acquire original works of art. In the years immediately leading up to 1909, J. P. Morgan and other trustees injected the Metropolitan with new energy and a greater sense of professionalism. Morgan enticed Sir Caspar Purdon Clarke and Wilhelm R. Valentiner to cross the Atlantic to serve as the Metropolitan's director and first curator of decorative arts respectively. Morgan, Clarke, and other museum trustees, administrators, and donors comprised the Celebration's art exhibition committee. It is little wonder that the Metropolitan Museum seized upon the Celebration as an opportunity to expand its reputation and its holdings.[8]

The Met mounted a pair of loan shows for its part in the Celebration. An exhibition of seventeenth-century Dutch painting represented Henry Hudson's world while galleries filled with American fine and decorative arts dating from the colonial and early national periods commemorated Robert Fulton. Each display was revolutionary in its own way.

Of the two exhibitions, the show of Dutch paintings received greater acclaim at the time. Rembrandt expert Wilhelm R. Valentiner gathered portraits, landscapes, still lifes, and religious and genre paintings emblematic of the golden age of art in the Netherlands, an era that coincided with Dutch rule in New Netherland. As with other aspects of the Celebration, organizers and reporters relied on a numerical tally to describe the show's importance. Their impressive reckoning of paintings totaled 149, including twenty by Frans Hals, five by Vermeer, and thirty-four by Rembrandt van Rjin. During the run of the exhibition, only the Hermitage in Saint Petersburg (then called Petrograd) could boast of a greater concentration of Rembrandts.[9]

At a time when only a handful of art museums existed in the United States, this display of Dutch Master paintings was extraordinary. Without exaggeration, writers here and abroad touted its magnitude. *The New York Times* reported that the exhibition would rival "any loan collection ever held in Europe." The *New-York Tribune* called it "about the most important event in the history of art in this country." Natalie Curtis writing in *The Craftsman* magazine stated that "the collection of Dutch paintings . . . has never been equaled in this country." German, English, and American art magazines reviewed the exhibition as well. Loan exhibitions of this size were rare even in Europe.[10]

Almost as intriguing as the paintings were their owners, art-loving American millionaires like Henry Clay Frick, George Jay Gould, Mrs. H. O. H. Havemeyer, Mrs. C. P. Huntington, and P. A. B. Widener. Their immense wealth permitted them to pursue their passion with vigor. Leading the way was the financier J. P. Morgan, a voracious collector who had amassed a treasury of manuscripts, old master drawings, early books, and paintings. The chairman of the joint art and historical exhibition committee of the Celebration as well as president of the Metropolitan Museum, Morgan gave $25,000 to support the show and loaned eight paintings.[11]

The Dutch paintings exhibition was a flashpoint. It trumpeted the fact that American connoisseurs with vast fortunes were rocking the European art world. It also coincided with the passage of the Payne-Aldrich Act and its repeal of a twenty-percent tariff on antique art imported into the United States. With the removal of this barrier, American collectors would become even more active and acquisitive. Lamenting the loss of treasures to American capitalists, the British National Gallery mounted a "protest" exhibition that ran concurrently with the Metropolitan's Dutch Masters show. In an article in Britain's *Burlington Magazine* American artist Kenyon Cox noted that the drain of great art was a pity for Europeans, but was a boon for the American public because the majority of these art treasures would, sooner or later, be donated to museums for all to enjoy.[12]

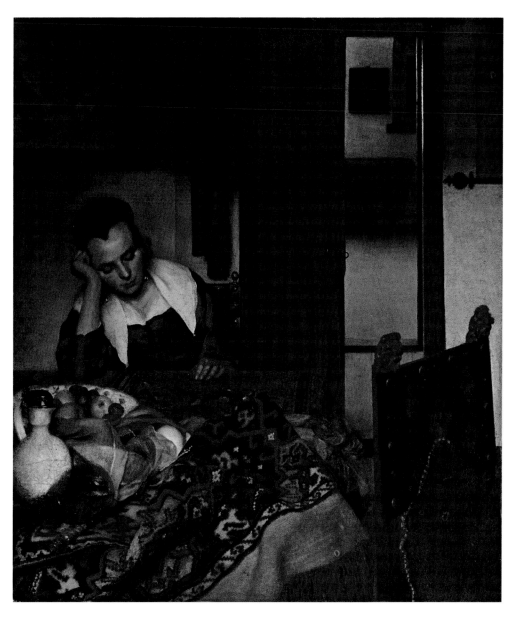

At the time, one collector's grandstanding really stood out. Less than a week before the exhibition opening, *The New York Times* received word from London that department store owner Benjamin Altman had just purchased a number of Rembrandts and other Dutch paintings from Duveen Brothers in London. With considerable swagger, this merchant-prince of New York placed six canvases in the exhibition at the last minute. Because of their late arrival, his trophy paintings hung together in one room rather than being interspersed among the other canvases—an installation with impact.[13]

Johannes Vermeer's "A Maid Asleep" was one of the canvases on view

Industrial Work for Public Schools (1904)

American arts exhibition at the Metropolitan Museum in 1909

The Metropolitan's "Hudson-Fulton Exhibition of American Industrial Arts" received less fanfare at the time, but is now considered a milestone in the history of American museums. Robert W. de Forest, chair of the art exhibition subcommittee of the Celebration, oversaw the first joint exhibition of American fine and decorative arts mounted by an art museum.[14] Prior to this exhibition, such family heirlooms and antiquarian curiosities were not highly and widely appreciated for their aesthetic qualities. This exhibition tested whether or not these objects could meet the criteria for true art. In 1909, Americans were poised to appreciate "industrial arts," a term they understood to mean objects made using hand tools and simple machines. With the popularity of the arts and crafts movement, children and adults were carving wood, hammering metals, and decorating pottery in school, settlement house, and home workshops. During this era of intense interest in colonial America, many were fascinated by the artistic skills and daily lives of their collective predecessors.

The exhibition, which featured objects belonging to Eugene Bolles and other early collectors, showcased colonial and early national period paintings, furniture, metals, ceramics, glass, and textiles. The curators' ecumenical approach extended beyond objects made in New York to include artifacts from

New England, Pennsylvania, and even Europe. Although generally well received, the industrial arts exhibition met with some mixed reviews. One critic noted that while there was "much to be learned by a careful study of . . . industrial arts," he could not help but observe that examples of Hepplewhite and Sheraton style furniture "had their very bad moments" with "chunky shield backs . . . hideous to contemplate." Another article bore the unsurprising subtitle "Early American School of Painting Makes a Meager Showing Compared with the Dutch Schools." While reviewer Natalie Curtis agreed that the Dutch Masters overshadowed early American painters, she praised the early American silver and furniture on display, noting how "instinctively the craftsmen of the humble Colonies sought simplicity of form and motive. Indeed, one is struck throughout the exhibition by the element of refinement and good taste, the absence of display, and the dignity of line and curve that characterize Colonial workmanship." Robert de Forest and his compatriots saw the exhibition as a test of Americans' interest in the

Portrait of Frederick Philipse by Gilbert Stuart, 1793–95

This portrait of an early New Yorker is visible in the photograph on the opposite page.

art history of their own country, and the warm reception of these American arts inspired the creation of the permanent display of American art and artifacts. Immediately after the close of the exhibition, at the behest of de Forest, Mrs. Russell Sage purchased the nearly 900 objects in the Bolles Collection for the Metropolitan Museum. These artifacts served as the core collection of the museum's American Wing when it opened fifteen years later.[15]

Over 300,000 artists, art lovers, and members of the general public visited the Metropolitan Museum during the exhibitions' two-month run, an enormous number for the period. Visitors included the social realist painter John Sloan, who visited the Dutch paintings exhibition multiple times, and art collector and future founder of the Museum of Modern Art, Abby Aldrich Rockefeller, whose father, Senator Nelson Aldrich, was one of the authors of the Act that had recently removed the tariff on imported art.[16]

Progressive-minded organizers were keen to document the success of the exhibitions, publishing statistics indicating the length of each exhibition's run, its square footage, and number of visitors. While there was some interest among organizers in gauging "the moral effect these displays had upon the public,"[17] in the end they adopted a slightly less strident approach:

The various exhibitions aroused in the minds of the beholders a more lively understanding of the history and development of our city, and while delighting the eye, conveyed an important lesson in the very best and most effective way—that is, unconsciously. A population like ours is greatly in need of some powerful stimulation of this kind to weld together all of its heterogeneous elements.[18]

Monument dedicated to Margaret Corbin

Organizers honored Corbin, a Molly Pitcher-type figure, and other patriots who battled Hessian soldiers.

Historical and artistic tributes extended beyond museum walls, to points around the city and along the Hudson River. Often blending aesthetics, historical significance, and pride of place, these dedications took the form of public sculpture and public parks. Within the city, organizations unveiled plaques and busts honoring people, events, and even structures from New York's past. Honorees included not only Hudson and Fulton, but also the seven teachers who taught in New York public schools during the period of Dutch occupancy; Margaret Corbin, a rather surprising candidate for Revolutionary War heroine who fought at Fort Tryon in northern

Manhattan; Giovanni da Verrazano, the first European known to have explored New York Harbor; and the sites of Fort Amsterdam (termed "The Cradle of the Metropolis" by organizers), New Amsterdam's city wall, and the Battle of Washington Heights.[19]

COPYRIGHT 1909 BY HARPER & BROS.

HUDSON MEMORIAL MONUMENT   HUDSON MEMORIAL BRIDGE

Postcard of the Hudson memorial monument and bridge as planned at the time of the Celebration

One of the most elaborate legacy projects planned was the Henry Hudson Memorial at Spuyten Duyvil. Hudson was associated with this place, where the northernmost tip of Manhattan Island meets the Bronx, based on an entry in the *Half Moon*'s log. Near here, Hudson's crew fought with armed natives in canoes, resulting in the death of several Indians. A bridge for carrying automobile traffic between the two boroughs, and to be named for the explorer, had been proposed in 1902. The city seriously studied the project, but a high cost estimate forced officials to table it. In 1906, Celebration organizers moved to resurrect the concept of constructing the bridge, now planned with a columnar monument honoring Hudson in a plaza at its

Ceremonial trowel used to lay the cornerstone of the Hudson monument

Harper's Weekly,
July 11, 1903

THE NEW HENDRIK HUDSON MEMORIAL BRIDGE

Plans have just been completed for the construction of a new bridge at Spuyten Duyvil, New York. It is to be built as a memorial to Hendrik Hudson, the first white man to sail up the river which bears his name. The bridge will be finished and opened to the public in September, 1909, the three-hundredth anniversary of Hudson's discovery.

north end. There was no more avid supporter of the project than William C. Muschenheim, Celebration organizer, host of the Celebration's official banquet at his establishment the Hotel Astor, and the man who happened to own the land in the Bronx where the bridge would be erected. Alas for Muschenheim, his dream met with obstacles. Although dignitaries dedicated the monument's cornerstone during the Celebration, it took decades for the project to be completed. The Henry Hudson Bridge did not open for traffic until 1936 and the monument was not completed until 1938.[20]

Across the Hudson River from Spuyten Duyvil, civic leaders also dedicated the Palisades Interstate Park as part of the Celebration. The effort to save the Palisades had begun in earnest in 1900 when members of the Federated Women's Clubs of New Jersey and other concerned citizens united to preserve this picturesque and geologically old mountain range. Quarry owners had chipped away at the mountains for centuries, but by the late nineteenth century miners were blowing the face off the Palisades using dynamite. (New York City builders used this distinctive sandstone to construct townhouses that came to be known as "brownstones.") To stop the desecration, these preservationists raised money and awareness to buy up thirteen miles of land from Fort Lee, New Jersey, to Piermont, New York, for the creation of a public park. Both New Jersey and New York legislatures provided some funds, as did the Women's

The Palisades of the Hudson (1909)

Clubs and a number of individuals, including white knight J. P. Morgan who gave the remaining $125,000 when it looked as if the deal would fall through.[21]

At festivities held in a colonial structure that was once the headquarters of Lord Cornwallis during the Revolution, the Governors of New Jersey and New York and George Kunz—a leader in the fight for the Palisades, gemologist at Tiffany's, president of the American Scenic and Historic Preservation Society, and chair of the Celebration's historical exhibition committee—spoke about the many values of preserving this land so close to the city. They recognized its historical significance, its immense beauty, the wise use of natural resources (including fresh air, green space, and clean water near the city), and the health and recreational opportunities it offered urban dwellers. Saving the scenic jewel of the Palisades for posterity expressed the highest hopes of the citizens of the Metropolis.[22]

In the Celebration equation, rich holdings of art and artifacts equaled imperial city status. Organizers dismissed the usual world's fair formula of constructing temporary exposition buildings filled with the latest machinery and consumer goods. Instead, they urged museums to mount Celebration-themed exhibitions as a way of helping assure institutional viability over the long term. Some, like the Metropolitan Museum of Art, attracted record crowds and new donors. With J. P. Morgan leading the charge, wealthy American connoisseurs showed off their European art trophies while demonstrating their belief in collecting for the benefit of the American public. Similarly, colonial-revival enthusiasts loaned their treasures to the first exhibition of American art and antiques at an art museum. The urge to memorialize extended beyond museum galleries to include public sculpture and other legacy projects. The Hudson-Fulton Celebration helped lay the foundation for the emergence of New York as an international center of art later in the twentieth century. ❖

Iroquois participating in the dedication of the Palisades Interstate Park

OFFICIAL PROGRAM

HUDSON-FULTON CELEBRATION

PRICE TWENTY-FIVE CENTS

Symbols, Souvenirs, & Sales

"PLEASURE AND ENTERTAINMENT WILL BE THE ORDER OF THE DAY DURING THE HUDSON-FULTON CELEBRATION / Very likely you have invited some friends and relatives from out of town to visit you during this occasion, and of course you are planning to make their visit an enjoyable one. Could anything provide better entertainment and amusement than a Sterling Player Piano. . . ."

Advertisement in *The Sun*, September 22, 1909

A world's fair without souvenirs? Unthinkable! Beginning with the first international fair, London's Crystal Palace Exposition of 1851, visitors considered souvenir shopping an essential part of the experience. By the time of the Hudson-Fulton Celebration, fifty years and countless expositions later, merchants tempted tourists with a dazzling array of mementos. Some commemoratives were officially licensed, highly symbolic, and dignified while others were bootleg, garish, and playful. In New York City, where mass merchandising and creative advertising were already part of the retailer's art, enterprising manufacturers and shopkeepers linked all kinds of products to the festivity, even if there were little or no connection. Using "Celebration fever" as a way to attract happy throngs to showrooms and stores, they positioned their regular merchandise—including overcoats, player pianos, and Japanese novelties—as remembrances of the great occasion.[1] New York dangled the traditional and the tacky, the clever and the commonplace before Celebration attendees with money to spare.

Some of the commemoratives were elegant, others *avant garde*, still others flashy. They reflected the artistic styles then in vogue as well as the aims of their makers. The stateliest were objects created by fine artists expressly for the Hudson-Fulton Celebration Commission. They were made in a classical style called the Amer-

Official Celebration medal

Souvenir badge

left: **Official Celebration badge**

**Model for badge used by Newburgh
officials**

*Up and down the river, local commit-
tees created their own commemoratives inspired by the Celebration's
official art.*

ican renaissance, popular at the time for government murals, monuments, and
other public art. This academic style based on ancient Greco-Roman design sig-
nified importance of purpose and eternalness of ideals. To twenty-first-century
viewers, the style can be a little disconcerting as artists sometimes mixed people, symbols, and scenery from both ancient and more recent eras. In contrast
to this conservative official art, the unauthorized souvenirs were far more lively
and eye-catching. Some merchandise was in the arts and crafts style, a modern,
slightly abstracted look that played on the historical and was very popular at the

time among graphic artists and decorative arts designers. By 1909, the once-popular Victorian style had been relegated to inexpensive goods. Manufacturers melded the style's ornate curves with mass production techniques to produce glitzy trinkets at a modest price. These tinny knick-knacks contrasted sharply with the objects of noble design the Commission had ordered.

Design was a point of contention. Souvenir vendors simply wanted to put forward attention-grabbing, saleable merchandise. They were not in the business of tutoring taste. Commission members, on the other hand, realizing that New York would be judged by the art and artifacts produced in conjunction with the Celebration, wanted to keep the design of commemoratives on the highest plane possible. They struggled with what they perceived as the crassness of commercialism associated with world's fairs. Hoping to prove that New York was much more than a money machine, Hudson-Fulton officials gave artists the mandate to create commemoratives that conveyed moral import.

Launching a design program was one of the Commission's early acts. Believing that "high art" possessed the power to inspire the beholder, the Commission authorized a series of official artifacts that included a medal, poster, flag, and badge.[2] In their design campaign, these civic leaders favored formality over inventiveness. They engaged academically trained, established artists and adopted a highly deliberate approach.

The Austrian sculptor Emil Fuchs, under the direction of the American Numismatic Society, created a prototype medal. On one side, Fuchs depicted Hudson addressing his crew on the deck of the *Half Moon*. During the design phase, Fuchs changed the scene repeatedly as scholars discovered more information about the historical details depicted. On the medal's reverse, Fuchs created a more broadly heroic, rather than period-specific, homage to Fulton. He placed women in classical dress, one with a miniature *Clermont* in hand, before a bust of the artist-inventor. This medal served as the prototype for thousands of cast versions in different sizes and alloys. Tiffany & Co. struck a small number of gold medals for leaders of nations who sent warships to New York, the major international patrons, as it were, of the Celebration. The firm Whitehead & Hoag minted all the others. The Commission designated silver medals for Commission members, local committee officials, guest dignitaries, and winners of aquatic events. Silver-plated, bronze, and aluminum versions were sold in department stores and given away as awards and keepsakes. The medal was promoted as "THE official souvenir."[3]

Like the medal, the poster mixed the allegorical and the strictly historical. When creating the Celebration's poster, the painter and muralist Edwin H. Blashfield put the classically clad "Spirit of Progress" center stage, flanking her

Postage stamp
Marcus Baldwin designed this early commemorative stamp issued on September 25, 1909.

Title page of official program
The Celebration's authorized publisher, Redfield Brothers, drew inspiration from antique book design.

with the figures of Hudson and Fulton in historical dress. In her striding step, winged headgear, and ship model she holds aloft, the goddess-like "Spirit" symbolized innovation in transportation. This theme fit the poster's final destination: most of the 78,000 posters printed were sent to railroad stations for the enjoyment of travelers.[4]

Other products also underscored the Commission's conservative approach. The flag, of which there were an estimated four to five million manufactured, incorporated the Celebration's official colors of orange, light blue, and white.[5]

This striking color scheme, inspired by the colors of the flag of the Netherlands under which Henry Hudson had sailed in 1609, dominated products and décor, with red, white, and blue a close second. The Stars and Stripes and the Celebration's banner were the only flags allowed on the streets of New York during the event. This was a source of contention among some foreign and some native participants, but the Commission's message was clear. International participation was warmly welcomed, but there could be no confusion over which nation's flag to salute.[6]

The official badges created by the Metallic Art Company followed in this serious vein and possessed a decidedly military flavor. The Commission crafted a fairly elaborate scheme wherein interchangeable medals, backs, bars, colored ribbons, and fringe indicated the different roles, responsibilities, and status of

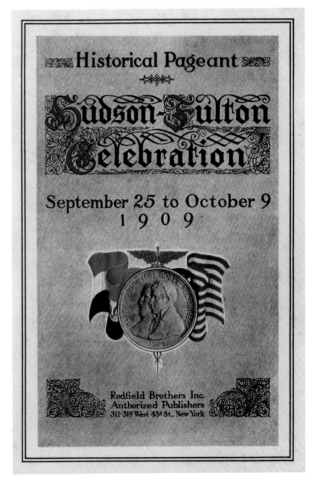

Cover and title page of official History Parade booklet

Cover and title page of *Manhattan* and *Henry Hudson* (1910)

In contrast to the Celebration's conservative graphics, the volume Dard Hunter designed shows a debt of gratitude to Viennese arts and crafts style.

Banquet plate

The importing firm of Lewis Strauss and Sons created a special dinner service for the 1,900 guests who attended the Celebration's official dinner at the Hotel Astor. The ballroom's elaborate décor was designed to evoke "a palace finished in Delft china."

the wearer, whether a commissioner, official guest, aide, or member of one of the Celebration's fifty-one working committees.[7] The badge completed the Commission's line of official ceremonial and souvenir artifacts.

The series of authorized souvenir publications—the official program, Historical Pageant booklet, Carnival Pageant booklet, and a set of seventy-two postcards—was slightly less formal in style than the official artifacts. This may be due in part to graphic designers' preference for more modern styles coupled with the need to promote sales. In their desire to avoid grossly commercial influence, the Commission members restricted paid advertising in sanctioned publications. Apparently Redfield Brothers, the officially licensed publisher, felt financial pressure. In one advertisement, the firm pointedly knocked its competitors, warning readers "the market is flooded with worthless and misleading books having little bearing on this great Celebration." But this negative advertising did not save the day. Noting that sales of its publications had not been as brisk as anticipated, a disappointed Redfield Brothers renegotiated the royalties owed the Commission after the Celebration's conclusion.[8]

The rekindled interest in early New York sparked the publication of countless histories that were quite different in look from the licensed publications. These histories employed the more cutting-edge arts and crafts style. The designer Dard Hunter of the Roycroft Press rode the crest of Hudson-Fulton Celebration fever with *Manhattan and Henry Hudson* (1910). While not an official publication, the volume drew on

Postcard

two orations delivered at the official banquet held at the Hotel Astor, an ode written and delivered by Joseph I. C. Clarke and a speech delivered by New York Senator Elihu Root.[9] Its cover design featured a sailing ship, a symbol with meaning not only to Hudson-Fulton attendees, but also to devotees of the arts and crafts movement, who glorified pre-industrial technology. Violet Oakley also used the arts and crafts style on the cover of the 1909 *Westchester County Historical Pageant*, where she depicted an early New York couple dressed in cavalier costume. While owing more to seventeenth-century Netherlandish portraiture than to the dress actually worn in colonial New York, the scene is irresistible in its historical romance. These two publications represent innovative designs that blossomed beyond the boundaries of official printed commemoratives.

Arts and crafts style cover of the *Westchester County Historical Pageant* (1909)

Leather-covered album with burned decoration

This souvenir album filled with family photos was found in Germany in 2005. Perhaps a sailor stationed aboard one of the four warships Germany sent to the Celebration purchased it during his 1909 stay in New York.

Postcard

Even though flags representing nations other than the United States were banned at the Celebration's public events, here the flag of the Netherlands hangs alongside the Stars and Stripes.

Unauthorized souvenirs made up in inventiveness what they might have lacked in design and production value. Manufacturers created mugs, felt pennants, printed handkerchiefs, pencils, novelty buttons, pocket wrenches, photograph albums, trading cards and other wares of varying quality, artistic merit, and price. Critics worried that many remembrances did not possess redeeming design value. A Dutch newspaper reporter's observations were typical. In more than one dispatch he noted the lack of taste in the souvenirs, citing that the sailing vessels depicted on some postcards and tiles had no relation to the supposed subject, the *Half Moon*. A reporter for *The New York Times* took a more sociological perspective. He saw the proliferation of Hudson-Fulton souvenirs as a logical outgrowth of the new banquet-favor industry. In his opinion, the recently developed companies that produced novelties for ballroom dinners hosted by business, charitable, and fraternal organizations had easily expanded their lines to fill this niche. He explained that the explosion of Hudson-Fulton keepsakes of varying quality should not be a surprise. It was an expected sign of the times.[10]

Celebration-related commerce moved beyond the realm of the traditional souvenir. During the fall of 1909, advertisements, displays, and promotions for nearly every product and service offered in New York referenced the Celebration in design, decoration, or simply "spirit." There were Hudson-

Postcards

A fanciful view of the Naval Parade is paired with an example
from the official History Parade float series.

Turkey Red Cigarette trading cards, Hudson-Fulton series

Fulton Celebration zithers, sheet music, and cigars for sale. Purveyors of clothing, field glasses, and groceries ran Hudson-Fulton Sales Days. On a slightly higher plane, Bloomingdale's invited out-of-towners to use their store as their "headquarters" during the festivities while Abraham & Straus in Brooklyn mounted a historically themed poetry contest for school children. A clothier staged "American Belles Through a Century in Fashion" in "living mode"—in other words, a fashion show. One reporter gleefully surveyed store windows that captured the spirit, if not the historical accuracy, of the Celebration. He pointed out curiosities such as the model of a mid-nineteenth-century sailing ship that was supposed to depict the far earlier *Half Moon*, the random artifact in the form of an old cannonball from Italy, and a hair restoration product's "before and

Cigar box label

Souvenir silver
teaspoon by
Tiffany & Co.

Sheet music for the *Hudson-Fulton Celebration March and Two-Step*

after" demonstrated on portraits of Hudson and Fulton. Perhaps most notable was the papier-mâché bologna, termed the "Illuminated Sausage," in a delicatessen window, a reference to the nighttime illumination of city landmarks as part of the Celebration.[11]

While the Commission hired artists to fashion artifacts that epitomized the Celebration's high ideals, other New Yorkers' aims were less lofty. Unlike Hudson-Fulton Celebration officials, ordinary businesspeople were not driven to rectify the city's image. To the contrary, they saw no conflict in honoring the spirit of history while making money. They happily mixed the commercial with the commemorative. If their attempts to sell merchandise sometimes took a comically strange turn, it made the Celebration all the more fun. ❖

Air & Sea,
Peace & War

"The two vessels, old fashioned and clumsy, were followed by such a merchant fleet as never before had been marshaled in parade in these waters, and they passed by a line of warships that told the story of the fighting strength of the navies of the world in terms of the most impressive significance."

New York Call, September 27, 1909

"I am rather planning to skip automobiles and take to flying machines, they look so comfortable and peaceful."

John D. Rockefeller, Jr., to Laura Spelman Rockefeller, October 5, 1909

To New Yorkers in the fall of 1909, the ship symbolized the past, present, and future. Hudson's *Half Moon* and Fulton's *Clermont*, and the marine construction and mechanics they represented, served as points of comparison for more recent technological achievements. While New Yorkers might not have envisioned the full extent of transportation developments during the twentieth century—super highways and super trains, ubiquitous commercial air travel, and rocket trips to and from the moon—they realized a new era was dawning. New York Harbor, though still the busiest in the world, was losing some share to other American ports and witnessing a decline in its ship-building industry. Hudson River steamboats were also under siege, challenged by railroads and automobiles. Despite these changes, or perhaps because of them, ships were central to Celebration activities, from the opening day's Naval Parade to the concluding sail of the *Half Moon* and *Clermont* from Cohoes back down the Hudson to New York.[1]

It might seem that the Celebration's sea-and-land parades were especially crafted as the most appropriate means to honor sailors Hudson and Fulton, but such was not the case. Since the eighteenth century, New York party planners had exploited Manhattan's spectacular natural setting to stage maritime parades linked to land processions. Among the first and most memorable was

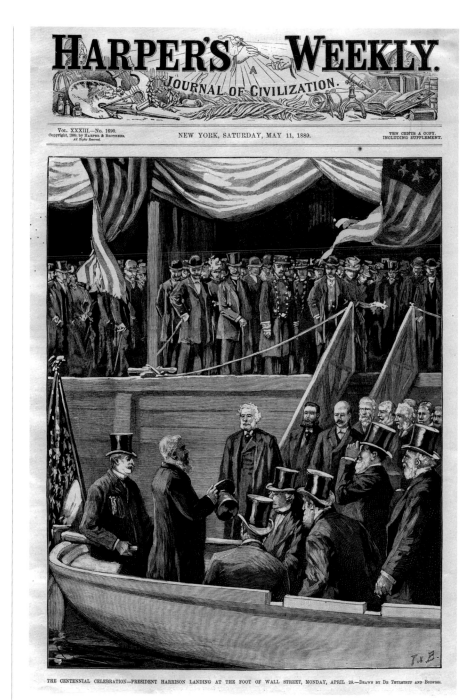

HARPER'S WEEKLY.

JOURNAL OF CIVILIZATION.

VOL. XXXIII.—No. 1690.
Copyright, 1889, by Harper & Brothers.
All Rights Reserved.

NEW YORK, SATURDAY, MAY 11, 1889.

TEN CENTS A COPY.
INCLUDING SUPPLEMENT.

THE CENTENNIAL CELEBRATION—PRESIDENT HARRISON LANDING AT THE FOOT OF WALL STREET, MONDAY, APRIL 29.—Drawn by De Thulstrup and Bogert.

President Harrison landing by boat during the commemoration of Washington's inauguration

The 1889 event depicted here marked the one-hundredth anniversary of George Washington taking the presidential oath of office and was one of many water and land festivals held in New York prior to the Hudson-Fulton Celebration.

George Washington's arrival to take the oath of office as president in 1789. As Washington approached Manhattan aboard a forty-seven-foot-long ceremonial barge, he was welcomed by a bevy of boats and sloops. After landing at the foot of Wall Street, he and his entourage proceeded to Cherry Street amidst cheering crowds and decorated buildings. Civic leaders employed the same general formula time and time again—to mark the Marquis de Lafayette's return visit (1824), the opening of the Brooklyn Bridge (1883), the centennial of British evacuation of the American colonies from New York (1883), the dedication of the Statue of Liberty (1886), the centennial of Washington's inauguration (1889), and the Columbian Celebration (1892). At the time of the Hudson-Fulton Celebration, New Yorkers recalled the most recent such festival—the victorious return of Admiral George Dewey from Manila Bay in the Philippines—and were invited to make comparisons, as when the *New York Herald* announced "Parade for Dewey Outdone by Far, Naval Demonstration Five Times Greater Than in New York Ten Years Ago."[2]

Stereoscope view of the *Half Moon*

The replica *Half Moon* depicted in seventeenth-century style

Replicas of the *Half Moon* and the *Clermont* embodied the eras and exploits of Hudson and Fulton. Spectators were particularly taken with Hudson's vessel, amazed that the tiny sailing ship was capable of crossing oceans. Ascertaining her design and construction had been somewhat difficult, since no plans or period images survived. Historians scoured First Mate Robert Juet's log, the plans of the *Half Moon*'s sister ship *Hope*, and other period sources showing similar craft. Based on plans drawn up by the Netherlands Navy Department, the Royal Shipyards in Amsterdam built the reproduction. Just shy of sixty feet from stem to stern, she was sixteen feet at her widest, and could carry eighty tons. Sails on the bowsprit, foremast, the mainmast, and mizzen-mast powered the vessel, allowing her to make seven knots when sailing before the wind. Two heavy guns were located at portholes on either side of the ship; two swivel guns on deck were used to return gun salutes

Design of the facsimile of the Half Moon.

Dutch sailors on the *Half Moon*

during the Celebration. The interior, as meticulously researched as the exterior, contained a hold, pantry, galley with fireplace, bread room, closets, sail room, sleeping berths, powder magazine, mate's cabin, and captain's cabin furnished with antiques. (School children touring the ship were particularly fascinated by Hudson's four-foot-high cabin.) The people of the Netherlands donated the replica *Half Moon*, constructed at a cost of $40,000, to the Hudson-Fulton Celebration Commission. The Holland-American Line steamship *Soestdyck* carried her from Amsterdam to the Brooklyn Navy Yard. There a Dutch specialist rigged and readied her for a crew of twenty from the Dutch warship *Utrecht*. As future events would reveal, these men were chosen for their short stature and ability to move around tight quarters rather than for skill in operating a ship with sails. They wore seventeenth-century style clothing when on board.[3]

Surprisingly, it was harder to document the appearance of Fulton's 1807 steamship than it was to determine the particulars of the seventeenth-century *Half Moon*. The *Clermont*, as the steamship came to be called long after its initial voyage, was a one-of-a-kind experimental craft. Fulton modified it almost immediately after its initial journey, and his own papers offered conflicting

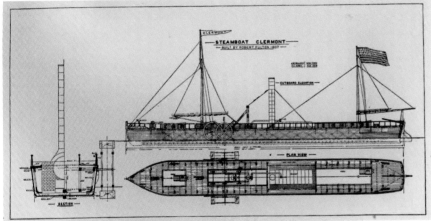

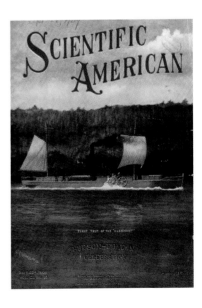

information about its design. American naval historians recreated the original craft, but made two alterations. They broadened the boat per Fulton's reworked design to improve stability and also painted "Clermont, New York" on her stern. The replica, constructed by the Staten Island Steamboat Company with funds provided by the Hudson-Fulton Celebration Commission, was one hundred and fifty feet long, nearly eighteen feet wide at the deck, and sixteen feet wide at the bottom. She was outfitted with a boiler, smokestack, single-cylinder engine, fly-wheels, paddlewheels and, as a back-up source of power, two mastheads for sails. She also carried the bell from the original *Clermont*. Like the *Half Moon*, the *Clermont* sported a colorful paint scheme, its overall gray-brown color enlivened by red paddlewheels and green engine trim. Descendants of Robert Fulton and Chancellor Robert Livingston, garbed in early-nineteenth-century style clothing, rode on the vessel during the Celebration. Chief among them was Alice Crary Sutcliffe, the author of a biography of her great-grandfather Robert

Rear view of the replica Clermont

The historical reenactors who rode onboard are visible in this detail from a 1909 photograph.

Steamship program

The Robert Fulton *was launched in 1909 in time for the Celebration.*

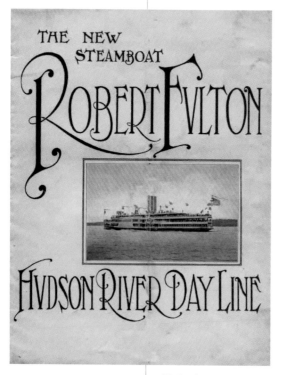

Fulton. Sutcliffe had christened the boat at its launch on July 10, 1909, with a bottle of well water from Livingston's home, Clermont, in honor of Fulton's disdain for ardent liquors.[4]

While the *Half Moon* suggested the age of sail in a general way, the *Clermont* stood for something more specific and New York-centric. During the Celebration, Empire State citizens relished the idea that the world was bowing to "Fulton's Folly" and its pioneering journey on the Hudson, a bona fide contribution to world history made in New York. Fulton's boat was the most renowned ancestor of steam-powered vessels. It was fitting that during the Celebration her offspring would come to call: pleasure yachts and steam launches; ferries that carried passengers between the boroughs and between New York and New Jersey; dayliners that plied the Hudson River, including the *Robert Fulton*, which was constructed especially for the Celebration; and even luxury ocean liners like the *Lusitania* and the *Nieuw Amsterdam*, in New York at the time of the event. Her grateful descendants also included battleships, cruisers, and other military watercraft representing England, Germany, France, Italy, the Netherlands, the Argentine Republic, Mexico, and the United States. Similarly, modern-day submarines and torpedo boats paid tribute to Fulton's trials with submarine and torpedo warfare. Proud New York progressives, delighting in the thought of how far maritime technology had advanced in one hundred years, took every opportunity to tie Fulton's experiments to present-day wonders.[5]

The opening day of the Hudson-Fulton Celebration, Saturday, September 25, featured a massive daytime Naval Parade followed by an illuminated nighttime show. The *Half Moon* and *Clermont* set out according to plan, sailing around New York Harbor accompanied by a few vessels for the enjoyment of millions standing on shore. But before they could get far into their journey, the wind grabbed the *Half Moon*'s sail and crashed her into the *Clermont*, causing the two to become entangled. Their crews separated them, a carpenter repaired the damage, and a tug captain took charge of the chastened *Half Moon*. In reality, only minor damage had occurred, but the incident took on epic proportions in newspapers hungry for drama. *The Evening Post* cried out "Half Moon Rams Clermont, Accident Mars Start of Great Naval Spectacle, Replica of Henry Hudson's Ship of Discovery, Unmanageable in the Face of Wind and Tide, Bore Down on Recon-

structed Steamboat—Crash Seen by Anxious Thousands" in an attempt to compete with an adjacent article about a dirigible explosion killing four in France. Most saw humor rather than pathos in the collision of the replicas. Social critic Gustave Kobbé considered the accident an amusing, and inauspicious, start to the festival. According to the *New York Press*, "everybody except members of the Hudson-Fulton Commission and those on the Half Moon and Clermont seemed to think it the best joke of the season."[6]

Comparison of the *Half Moon*, the *Clermont*, and the *Mauretania*

The Mauretania, *sister ship of the* Lusitania, *carried its first passengers in 1907. In September 1909, it made headlines by clocking the fastest westward crossing of the Atlantic Ocean, a record it held for nearly twenty years.*

Hudson River Naval Parade
Spectators packed excursion boats for a close-up view of the flotilla.

Water Gate Landing at 110th Street

The *Half Moon* and *Clermont* were soon back on course on their trip up the Hudson River. Like an elaborate dance, the replicas cruised in front of, among, and between squadrons of steamships, ferries, tugs, torpedo boats, submarines, steam yachts, motor boats, and tenders toward the "mightiest armada ever gathered in American Waters." Stretching from midtown to Spuyten Duyvil, a ten-mile-long column of American and foreign warships lay at anchor in the mid-

dle of the river. The replicas received a twenty-one-gun salute from the battle-ships before docking at the Water Gate Landing for speeches and presentations. In a highly choreographed maneuver, some of their escort squadrons sailed in a circle around the assemblage of warships. Crowds watched from skyscrapers and roofs, from Riverside Park and the Palisades, and from boats hired for the occasion. Eighty-seven warships and nearly 1,500 other vessels participated in this special Celebration rendezvous.[7]

Imaginary view of the Naval Parade

This centerfold from a commemorative booklet issued by the Lackawanna Railroad captures the spirit, if not the reality, of the flotilla. Some in the audience were disappointed that there was no single line of sail.

START OF THE GREAT PARADE UP THE HUDSON RIVER—HALF MOON, MANNED BY A CREW FROM HOLLAND IN THE COSTUMES OF HUDSON'S TIME, AND CLERMONT, WITH THOSE ON BOARD DRESSED AS THEY WERE A HUNDRED YEARS AGO, LEADING, FOLLOWED BY THE GREATEST BATTLESHIP FLEET EVER GATHERED TOGETHER IN AMERICAN WATERS

Even with all this pomp and show, some spectators were disappointed in the daytime event. There were those who took the phrase "Naval Parade" literally, assuming that all vessels, including the warships, would form a procession in a straight line. Some spectators objected that the *Half Moon* did not sail under her own power, but was pulled along by a tether, after her runaway accident. Others complained that seeing modern destroyers and submarines with the *Half Moon* and *Clermont* ruined the historical atmosphere.[8]

141

In the evening, the on-water party continued. Some of the Naval Parade maneuvers were repeated in the dark, with electric lights delineating the ships' shapes, searchlights sweeping, and fireworks exploding. This glittering display seemed to make any reservations about the daytime festivities fade:

Then by prearrangement at eight bells, the whole fleet burst into outlines of light, as if suddenly touched with the propitious augury of St. Elmo's Fire—the masts, decks, water lines, and other chief features glowing with thousands of sparkling electric globes. And for hours these ponderous, death-dealing machines, lying peacefully on the bosom of the Hudson in friendly association, scintillated like the airy fabrics of a magician or the unsubstantial dreams of an oriental fairy tale. It was a scene of exquisite beauty which will never be forgotten by the millions of people who thronged to the river side to see it.[9]

Illumination of warships during the Celebration

The artist John Sloan recorded in his diary that he was invited by Henry Reuterdahl to observe the opening day's Naval Parade from his house in Weehawken. According to Sloan, Reuterdahl was "the 'promptor' for this production. His article on the deficiencies of the Navy made a great stir last year or the year before."[10] President Theodore Roosevelt had encouraged Reuterdahl, a popular

Stereoscope view of the *Georgia*
In New York for the Celebration, this warship had participated in the Great White Fleet's recently completed sail around the world.

commercial artist specializing in marine subjects, to sail with the Great White Fleet on its around-the-world tour. When the American warships set off in October 1907 with Reuterdahl on board, Roosevelt did not know that the artist had written an article critical of American battleship construction and gun installation for *McClure's Magazine.* When the article was published a few months later, Roosevelt was so angry that he ordered the artist put off ship immediately. Reuterdahl, who had to find his way home from Chile, clearly had touched a nerve. Early in the twentieth century, naval might was associated with international standing and important nations invested heavily in state-of-the-art warships. This strategy had been encouraged by American Alfred Thayer Mahan's internationally popular book *The Influence of*

Celebration postcard

Sea Power Upon History (1890) as well as by lessons learned during the Spanish-American War (1898) and the Russo-Japanese War (1904–1905). Leading naval powers England and Germany were caught up in an escalating arms race, England having raised the stakes with the launching of the *Dreadnought* (1906), a vessel so advanced that it sparked a new class of battleship, represented at the Celebration by the *Inflexible.*[11]

The Naval Parade committee, composed of military officers as well as civilians, arranged for the proper reception of, and logistics for, foreign and American naval vessels. The United States wanted to use the military gathering of ships at the Hudson-Fulton Celebration to thrust itself into the company of England and Germany, but this assertion posed problems. America's navy was not yet in their league (the nicest thing German Grand Admiral von Koester could say was that the American fleet was the only one that had sailed around the world), but the United States wanted to display its fighting power and wartime readiness anyway, particularly after Reuterdahl's article. The United States recognized heightened political tensions between the two European nations, yet it did not want to choose sides between its mother country and the homeland of millions of German Americans.[12]

Political allegiances aside, many Americans were mesmerized purely on mechanical terms by these behemoths and the advancements in technology they represented. During the Naval Parade, the most curious hired launches and rowboats to get them within thirty feet of the large ships. They also had access to most American and foreign warships on visiting days. The socialist newspaper the *New York Call*, disapproving of the public's fascination with battleships, sarcastically observed that "Visitors Like Murder Boxes."[13]

Socialists were not alone in their displeasure. Members of the League of Peace, the American Peace Society, and other groups protested the opening day's Naval Parade. Edwin D. Mead of the Peace Society deplored such an arms show at a festival honoring commercial life while *The Evening Post* opined before the event that "our celebration has to do with the arts and inventions of peace, and yet the most prominent feature of it is to be the death-hurling instruments of war. . . . Perhaps some day popular excitement

Postcard of Military Parade

Newspapers reported that this was the first time armed foreign troops had marched in New York since the Revolutionary War.

Fold-out Celebration sou-
venir showing sky and
water craft sailing up the
Hudson

and enthusiasm may be aroused by an art exhibition such as that of the Dutch paintings in the Metropolitan Museum, which really meant something to civilized humanity." Celebration organizers tried to walk the line between these camps by positioning the Hudson-Fulton event as a tribute to peace, and New York as a neutral, happy place for the officers, soldiers, and marines from different nations to meet. They arranged for entertainments ranging from formal receptions to rowing races, from theater shows to free passes on the IRT, to encourage international camaraderie.[14]

On September 30, the crews of these ships joined American soldiers and militia units in a mammoth land parade. Like the Naval Parade, this street procession prompted a range of responses concerning military build-up. Using the superlative-laden language of the day, *The New York Times* proclaimed "Millions Cheer Martial Pomp, City's Biggest Crowd Drawn by Marching of the Fighting Men of the Nations, Best of Fulton Pageants, Twenty-five Thousand Men in Line and 2,250,000 Looking On—Miles of Uniforms, Ovation for Kaiser's Men, Historic 'Goose-Step' Catches the Multitude—Cheers for Businesslike Britons—Fine Showing of Cadets." *The Evening Post* stated that "the absence of large bodies of regular soldiers [in the United States] was a striking feature of the parade . . . the splendid example of a country really unarmed on land still survives, despite the mania for battleships." Prior to the Celebration, the *New York Call* lamented that a parade composed of "thousands of uniformed man killers" would be a central event, while the *Daily People* remarked that the parade offered "a saddening sight when one thought of all the intelligent, able-bodied men withdrawn from productive industry and furnished with death-dealing weapons solely for the purpose of shooting down their brothers in defence [*sic*] of their respective capitalist interests."[15]

A NEW KIND OF GULL IN NEW YORK HARBOR

Wilbur Wright, who was under contract to give demonstrations with his aeroplane during the Hudson-Fulton celebration, made a most spectacular flight on September 29th, when he circled the Statue of Liberty in New York Harbor, and returned to the starting-point on Governors Island without mishap, reaching a speed of fifty miles an hour

"Sky sailors" and "sky craft" caused less controversy and even more exhilaration. When planning the Celebration, organizers decided that flight along the Hudson River by dirigibles and airplanes would be the perfect climax to its survey of three hundred years of transportation. Postcards and commemorative plates featured Verneian views of airplanes and dirigibles gliding above the Hudson and watercraft of all sorts cruising below. While their plan to engage European zeppelin companies was not realized, Celebration organizers contracted with American pioneering aviators Wilbur Wright and Glenn Curtiss to show off their flying machines. Wright's flight would be his first purely public display, not an air show feature or a demonstration for business reasons. If this were not enough, the Wright Brothers were in the middle of a legal battle with Curtiss over patent infringement. The duel was on. The anticipation only intensified when the *New York World* established a $10,000 prize for the first person who replicated Fulton's journey by flying between New York and Albany.[16]

Flight fever ran high. One paper announced, erroneously as it turned out, that a zeppelin would be carrying sightseers around the city during the Celebration. Another described the combination airplane and dirigible that the Roeder Brothers had constructed in White Plains and hoped to enter in the *New York World* air race. The *New York Herald* teased "Hudson-Fulton Flights to Be the Most Perilous Ever Undertaken . . . Surprises are Promised" in an article illustrated by photographs of airplane crashes from the Rheims Air Meet. Wanamaker's department store announced that it would display the race-winning plane Glenn Curtiss had flown at Rheims, identical to the one he would be flying in New York. Since early aviators were dependent on perfect weather and wind conditions, organizers designed a code system of flags flown around the city that would offer up-to-the-minute postings about the "flight situation." [17]

Photograph of Wright standing by his plane
In his New York flying demonstrations, Wright was more successful than his rival. Curtiss made two trips during the Celebration, each lasting under a minute.

Alas, the weather was not cooperative. Most days were unsuitable for aeronautics. Wright's most extensive flight was a twenty-mile, half-hour trip from Governor's Island to Grant's Tomb and back in which he reached two hundred feet in altitude. Prior to this spectacular excursion, he had made two shorter trips, including a picturesque loop around the Statue of Liberty, a resounding crowd-pleaser. In a scene that seems poignant now, Wright navigated close to the *Lusitania* as she left for Europe, with departing travelers waving handkerchiefs on deck and the steam from her whistle rocking his airplane. New Yorkers found this taciturn Midwesterner who faced danger with such calmness intriguing. They loved spying the red canoe he had purchased in a Manhattan store and slung under his airplane in case of an emergency landing in water.[18]

Dirigible launch during the Celebration

Excited onlookers gathered to watch at a location near Grant's Tomb.

While aviators took advantage of whatever decent conditions came their way, on September 29, the *Half Moon* and *Clermont* left the 110th Street landing, getting a head start on the warships and other vessels that would join them in Newburgh a few days later. The *New York World* air race made its official start on the same day, with two entrants, both dirigibles, vying for the big money. The organizers' dream of an air-and-water flotilla moving upriver was realized—at least for a moment. Dirigible captains Baldwin and Tomlinson turned out not to be as successful as Fulton. Baldwin's dirigible fell into the Hudson River near 190th Street; Tomlinson limped into White Plains with oil and gas tanks leaking.[19]

Hudson-Fulton Celebration organizers grafted their event onto a formula of marine and land pageantry that New Yorkers had enjoyed for centuries. The emphasis on ships of all sorts underscored the relationship between the metropolitan port city of New York and the Hudson River, its major connection to the hinterland. The replicas of Hudson's *Half Moon* and Fulton's *Clermont* served as starting points for a technological revolution in travel and transport. Citizens of the Empire State were particularly proud of Robert Fulton's successful voyage in 1807, a New York first, and the variety of steam-powered craft that saw the *Clermont* as a valued forerunner. Among these were the battleships and other military vessels invited to assemble in the Hudson River as part of the Celebration's festivities. In an era when international importance was expressed through naval prowess, the United States wanted to showcase its fleet before participating nations. Powerhouses England and Germany might not recognize the United States as a military equal, but they could at least pay homage to the *Clermont* as an ancestor of the battleship and to Fulton as a father of modern naval warfare. Many found the Celebration's atmosphere of militarism inappropriate and frightening. In contrast, all New Yorkers were thrilled by the notion of Wilbur Wright, Glenn Curtiss, and other aviators soaring around the city and up and down the Hudson. Progressives saw air flight and its upward aspirations as a fitting ending to their homage to historic transportation. ❖

**Dirigible aloft during
the Celebration**

*With St. John the Divine
under construction in the
background, sightseers
crane their necks to see
a dirigible in flight.*

Hudson, Fulton
Day Albany Oct. 8.
1909. 205

Scene Albany Harbor
Hudson Fulton
Day Oct 8 09

Two scenes of Hudson
River festivities in Albany

Up the River

"Our *Hudson-Fulton* Celebration opening Oct 7th when our city gay with bunting and flags gave itself over to the entertainment and enjoyment of its guests is so recent and so fresh in our memories that comment seems superfluous. The parades—anchoring of the Half Moon, Clermont & battleships in the river opposite our city—the salutes fired—the addresses given by Gov. Hughes & others at the unveiling of the monument given by the D.A.R. and the Sons of Columbia—the floats representing the different epochs in our national history—the handsome lunch given our distinguished guests in our Chapter House, the picturesque effect of our nightly illuminations are now a matter of history upon which we reflect with natural pride & pleasure. In reviving the past, the fires of patriotism have been kindled anew, and with pardonable pride we recall the progress of our nation, past & present—and its glorious promise of the future."

M. O. Folger, Historian's Report, City of Hudson Chapter
of the Daughters of the American Revolution

Hudson-Fulton Celebration holiday-making did not stop in Manhattan, but proceeded on to Brooklyn, the other boroughs, and Hudson River cities and towns. In the river towns especially, the commemoration unfolded over a series of days and featured the typical small-town menu of fireworks, parades, dedications, concerts, church services, speeches, and banquets. Members of the Commission's planning and scope committee coordinated the overall schedule and shared some big-city elements. They arranged for the *Half Moon* and *Clermont* to anchor near selected towns on pre-assigned days. They divided up the floats that had ornamented Manhattan's History of New York Parade into two mobile units and contracted with a private carrier to take them from town to town on barges for use in local processions. They engaged the Iroquois dancers and musicians who had first appeared in Manhattan to participate in the town parades, traveling on a houseboat-type barge along with the floats. Similarly, Governor Charles Evans Hughes delivered stirring speeches in cities, towns, and villages all along the Hudson. Corporate-style orchestration and

Official viewing stand in Albany

enhancements notwithstanding, these local festivals possessed their own flavor and a quality of authenticity. These festivities, mounted by local citizens' committees, strengthened the bonds of community, and business, along the scenic corridor of the Hudson River.

Manhattan may have been the main theater for New York City's festivities, but Brooklyn, Staten Island, the Bronx, and Queens also mounted their own fêtes. Brooklyn's commemoration days were the most ambitious, but also the most fraught with trouble. In particular, Brooklyn's History of New York and Carnival Parades, envisioned as large-scale processions incorporating all of the floats that had debuted in Manhattan, met with a series of mishaps. Even before

Celebration in Albany

the Celebration had begun, officials discovered that 5,000 highly coveted tickets for grandstand seats were missing, prompting a fight among Brooklyn aldermen that resulted in broken furniture and embarrassing coverage in the newspapers. This unfortunate affair was followed by a failure in parade planning. Those in charge of logistics did not realize that the tall floats would not be able to travel under Brooklyn's low-hanging trolley wires. By the time IRT workers had cut the wires to facilitate parade formation, irreparable confusion had set in. Crews never even unloaded half of the floats from their barges, forcing St. Nicholas to ride in a buggy and Henry Hudson to walk. (The floats would continue to cause distress in towns upriver when they arrived too late or badly damaged.) If this were not enough, Brooklyn's Carnival Parade narrowly averted true disaster. Set on fire by a Roman candle or a gasoline torch, one of the papier-

mâché floats went up like a match, forcing little girl fairies to jump nine feet to the pavement to escape the flames. Happily, an evening literary program and a ball held at the Brooklyn Academy of Music went off without incident.[1]

In the other boroughs, the festivities were more successful. On Staten Island, the historical parade, incorporating half of the floats used in Manhattan, came together according to plan. The borough's day-long program of oratory and song included the unusual feature of women speakers. While women at the podium may seem utterly conventional today, the spectacle of Miss Mary Wolcott Green delivering an address on behalf of the Daughters of the American Revolution and Mrs. Ira K. Morris reciting "The Graves of the Huguenots" represented a rarity during the Celebration. The Bronx mounted the largest parade in its history to date, having hosted an elaborate banquet for dignitaries the night before. On October 6, each of the five wards in Queens mounted a special program of speeches, music, and fireworks.[2]

As Manhattan was easing up on the throttle at the end of the Celebration's first week, towns along the Hudson were just gearing up. Organizers designated October 1 as Hudson River Day, the official kick-off for merrymaking north of New York City. These river-town celebrations, organized and funded through a combination of state monies and private contributions, had a distinctive aura. The parades were less rigid and more inclusive than those mounted in the big city. Members of labor unions rode on floats and marched as escorts in places like Yonkers, Albany, and Peekskill, something not seen in Manhattan where organizers were uneasy about the power of

Marchers representing the Croton Manufacturing Company

Excluded from Celebration parades in Manhattan, labor unions and businesses participated in river-town processions.

labor and affiliated political parties.[3] In addition, community affirmation came easily in these small-town parades, where spectators knew those marching and vice versa. Many towns added their own floats—more personal and fun and often more attractive than the Mardi Gras-like concoctions redistributed from Manhattan's History Parade. Civic pride was heartfelt and uncomplicated, not imposed.

A case in point was Cornwall, on the west bank of the Hudson, where townsfolk mustered for a glorious all-American procession before 20,000 applauding spectators:

The parade in the morning was one of the most picturesque given along the river. It included members of the Grand Army [Civil War veterans] in coaches; one thousand school children representing the entire town of Cornwall, marching; members of the fraternal and patriotic societies with banners and uniformed as follows: Independent Order of Red

Staten Island banquet menu

Up and down the Hudson, Celebration banquets featured themed food, speeches, decorations, and even favors.

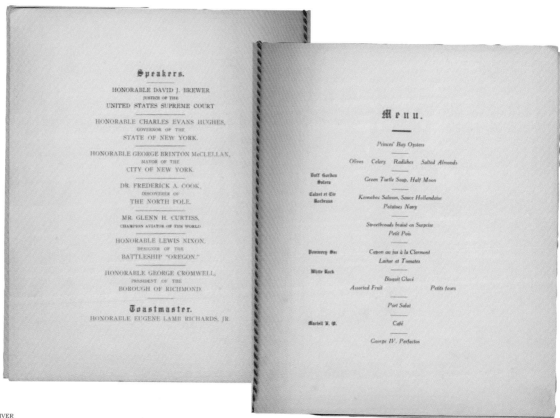

Speakers.

HONORABLE DAVID J. BREWER
JUSTICE OF THE
UNITED STATES SUPREME COURT

HONORABLE CHARLES EVANS HUGHES,
GOVERNOR OF THE
STATE OF NEW YORK.

HONORABLE GEORGE BRINTON McCLELLAN,
MAYOR OF THE
CITY OF NEW YORK.

DR. FREDERICK A. COOK,
DISCOVERER OF
THE NORTH POLE.

MR. GLENN H. CURTISS,
CHAMPION AVIATOR OF THE WORLD.

HONORABLE LEWIS NIXON,
DESIGNER OF THE
BATTLESHIP "OREGON."

HONORABLE GEORGE CROMWELL,
PRESIDENT OF THE
BOROUGH OF RICHMOND.

Toastmaster.
HONORABLE EUGENE LAMB RICHARDS, JR.

Menu.

Princes' Bay Oysters

Olives   Celery   Radishes   Salted Almonds

Doff Garden
Sutern   Green Turtle Soup, Half Moon

Culvet et Cie
Bordeaux   Kennebec Salmon, Sauce Hollandaise
                      Potatoes Navy

                      Sweetbreads braisé en Surprise
                      Petit Pois

Pommery Sec   Capon au jus à la Clermont
                      Laitue et Tomates

White Rock
                      Bisquit Glacé
Assorted Fruit   Petits fours

                      Port Salut

Martell V. O.   Café

                      George IV. Perfectos

Men, United Order of American Mechanics, Knights of Columbus, Patriotic Sons of America, Independent Order of Odd Fellows, Knights of Pythias, Foresters of America, Royal Arcanum, Independent Order of Foresters, Companions of the Forest, Mountainville Grange, Cornwall Club, Veterans of the Spanish-American War, and the Firthcliff Club; thirty ladies of the Order of the Pocohontas [sic] in the complete costumes of Indian squaws; Great Chief Bear in gorgeous native costume, accompanied by Red Men dressed as chieftains (all these wore original costumes of American Indians); Storm King Engine Company in full uniform; Highland Engine Company in full uniform; thirty-five ladies and children in native Indian costumes; seventy-five men in complete Indian dress of which twenty-five were mounted; twenty-five floats representing the degrees of advancement since the discovery of the Hudson; and one hundred and twenty-five cadets from the New York Military Academy of Cornwall-on-Hudson. The most beautiful floats represented the Dutch, Indian, Colonial, Patriotic, and Commercial subjects.[4]

Local citizens' committees also differed with the Manhattan-based Commission about the role of business in Celebration proceedings. The Commission was so concerned about the taint of the commercial that they earmarked its avoidance as a main goal. To Hudson Valley civic leaders, business boosterism was an unquestioned element of their programs. While their big-city cousins wanted to prove to the world that New York was interested in pursuits other than making money, Hudson Valley residents did not have that weight to bear. They welcomed businesses underwriting floats and publications. On America's main streets, remembrance and merchandise were completely compatible.[5]

Peekskill committee members

155

The Celebration speeches delivered in Hudson River towns reveal other differences between country and city. When in the Valley, aside from honoring local citizens and their accomplishments, orators paid kudos to the great state, rather than city, of New York. They also lauded the Hudson Valley—its scenic beauty, rich Revolutionary War history, and ample commercial opportunities. If they evoked the Metropolis at all, it was done so briefly and usually as a terminus of the Hudson River, that incomparable waterway. Even in the highly industrialized cities with immigrant populations, leaders did not talk about acculturation or the other burning concerns of New York City.[6]

Program of Events

The commercial met the commemorative in this advertisement for Moody's oyster and chop house. The concept of "Old Home Week" encouraged community reunions.

River towns linked their Hudson-Fulton commemorations to the idea of "Old Home Week," a yearly reunion concept which had developed in New Hampshire a decade earlier. This type of festival, usually held in the summer, was designed to counteract the brain drain taking place in rural and small-town America as ambitious young people left in search of greater opportunity. It was hoped that if bright young things returned to their hometowns for a week of fun, camaraderie, and community, they might be enticed to stay. Using this tack, organizers wanted to encourage those beyond the Hudson Valley to travel back for Celebration fun. Poughkeepsie's Old Home Week campaign included mailing press materials to newspapers across the country, distributing 10,000 invitational booklets, negotiating special railroad rates, and running an office to register returnees and to help them find lodging. Herbert Rankin, attending Princeton University at the time of the Celebration, was a perfect Old Home Week candidate. His father wrote him from Albany "you must let us know your plans and we shall be glad to see you and your friends if you come. Your mother and Eddie were very enthusiastic about the New York City display despite the crowd and they are rather turning up their nose at our poor attempts. I hear Troy is to be fine."[7]

As was fitting during community days, each town highlighted its own historical events and emphasized its special story. For example, Newburgh honored Palatine settlers who came in 1709 while residents of Albany reveled in their early and deep Dutch roots. While not exactly history, Catskill's theme was "Rip Van Winkle," a folkloric tale Washington Irving had set in the nearby Catskill Mountains. This focus on local historical flavor was nowhere more apparent than in Yonkers. Philipse Manor Hall, a masterpiece of colonial Georgian architecture and a seat of the Philipse family's 57,000-acre manor, served as the city's

Celebration emblem. Not only was the structure the subject of a float in Manhattan's History Parade, but it also represented the latest in historic preservation. For decades, it had served as the City Hall until Yonkers government had grown too large. New York State had acquired the structure in 1908 with financial support from Mrs. William F. Cochran and, working in partnership with the American Scenic and Historic Preservation Society, planned to restore and open it as a museum.[8]

The city and bay of Newburgh served as the centerpiece of Hudson River activities on October 1. Here, in a grand spectacle, the Celebration officially switched focus to the upper Hudson. The *Half Moon, Clermont*, and their escorts—having completed a tour of the lower Hudson—gathered at Cornwall, a few miles south of Newburgh. Meanwhile, eight squadrons of ships, boats, and other craft set out from the northern tip of Manhattan. As they swept up the Hudson, all eyes were on them, even at Sing Sing, where one thousand prisoners were permitted to gather in the yard to watch (but not to cheer).

**Naval Parade
at Newburgh**

Indeed, spectators from Manhattan to Newburgh lined the shores of the Hudson to witness a thrilling naval display that included the arctic ship *Roosevelt*, captained by Peary himself. The submarines, revenue cutters, warships, steamers, motorboats, and tugs eventually joined the historical vessels in Cornwall, and they sailed into the bay *en masse*. Newburgh's incomparable setting, with its wide bay and sloping hillside, provided a natural amphitheater for thousands of onlookers. With these ceremonies, the *Half Moon* and *Clermont* were officially turned over to the care of the upper Hudson committee. Some of the vessels continued north traveling with the replica ships, while others, especially those of a deep draft, sailed back to New York City.[9]

During the next week and a half, Hudson Valley cities, towns, and villages were joyous with history. Among the most involved were the doings in Yonkers, where there was a grand history parade involving an estimated 200,000 spectators, making it the biggest Celebration gathering outside of New York City. With residents of Mount Vernon and New Rochelle as well as Yonkers participating, representatives of local industries and labor unions marched alongside those from fire companies and volunteer organizations. Other Yonkers festivities included a civic parade of city workers, band concerts, school exercises, and boat races.[10]

Parade coming through ceremonial arch in Getty Square, Yonkers

Parade at Broadway and Main Street, Tarrytown

Elsewhere in Westchester County, and in Rockland and Putnam Counties, the commemorations were not as extensive but no less exciting for townspeople. A multi-village

parade marched along Broadway from Hastings to North Tarrytown (Sleepy Hollow) with fewer floats than expected, the Nyack Committee having hired a tug and stealthily carried off six for their own parade in the dead of night. Ossining, Croton, and Cold Spring mounted parades, as did Peekskill, the last second only to Yonkers in size in the lower Hudson Valley.[11]

The upper Hudson committee arranged for each of the major towns to enjoy a special day of commemoration during its period of celebration. Moving from south to north, Poughkeepsie marked its "great day" on October 4, Kingston on the 5th, Catskill on the 6th, Hudson on the 7th, Albany on the 8th, Troy on the 9th, and Cohoes on the 10th and 11th.[12] Staying true to the Old

Broadway sleigh float in the Peekskill parade

River-town parade
Legions of little girls dressed in white and carrying flags marched in Peekskill.

Parade participants in historical costume
These proud citizens of Peekskill rode on floats depicting the Broadway sleigh and George Washington's coach.

159

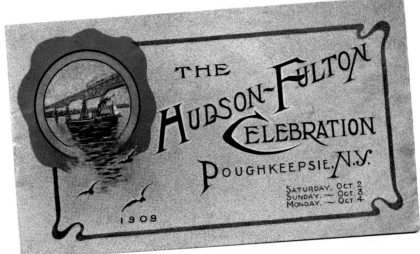

Home Week formula, each town's hoopla offered revealing glimpses into the world of 1909.

During Poughkeepsie's three-day event, 20,000 attended outdoor religious services and Vassar College students and naval officers hosted each other on campus and on warship. At Kingston, civic leaders dedicated a plaque to the city's founding father, Sir Thomas Chambers, at the Industrial Home, Ulster County's orphanage. To reach the Kingston festivities, Governor Hughes sped along on a torpedo boat from Poughkeepsie. It broke a Hudson River record by reaching twenty-six miles per hour. In Catskill, town officials dedicated a statue of Rip Van Winkle. Circa 1900, the iconic character enjoyed both local and

Governor Hughes in Catskill

A "living flag" on the steps of the Capitol in Albany

national popularity among the many Americans who felt that they, too, had suddenly awakened to a much changed world. In the city of Hudson, the Daughters of the American Revolution funded the city's first monument, a Hudson-Fulton memorial water fountain that served both small animals and people. In 1909, public water fountains were implicitly associated with the temperance movement in the United States.[13]

Albany took particular pride in the fact that it was the end point for both Hudson's and Fulton's journeys. In keeping with the era's growing fascination with militarism and the colonial revival, the city's history days included a United States Military Tournament with drills and demonstrations on Island Park and its own American fine and decorative arts exhibition at the Albany Institute of History and Art, the first major exhibition mounted at its new location on Washington Avenue. With the aid of the directors of the Rensselaer Polytechnic Institute, the city of Troy installed particularly lavish electrical and architectural decorations centered in its business district. Its historical fantasy included a large-scale, mechanized windmill with rotating arms outlined in lights. At a time when women did not yet have the right to vote in New York, Trojans designated

the only Women's Day during the Celebration, honoring the contributions made by female volunteer organizations, graduates of the Emma Willard School, and philanthropist Mrs. Russell Sage. On October 9, beacon fires, meant to "closely resemble the Pillars of Fire of Bible times," burned on Hudson Valley hilltops from Troy to Staten Island marking the culmination of the Celebration.[14]

Exercises at Cohoes served as a coda to the history affair and provided organizers the opportunity to reflect upon the Celebration as a whole. Governor

Celebration decorations in Troy

Hughes found the public school students he had encountered throughout the festivities particularly inspiring—"the promise of America." He was delighted that the Celebration encouraged a shared appreciation of American ideals among young people living in the northern reaches of the Hudson Valley as well as in New York City. President of the Commission Stewart Woodford noted that while he had been pleased to meet admirals and to see the navies of the world, he was most impressed by the 300,000 school children marching in Children's Day events in New York City. He cherished the memories of electrical illuminations and was moved by Manhattan's Military Parade as an expression of peace and good will. In his opinion, the people of the United States had presented themselves well to the world, participating in Celebration events "joyously yet seriously." Citing the progressives' beloved statistics, he remarked that the two weeks of commemoration were marked by little crime and very few accidents—and the death rate was the lowest it had been in thirty years![15]

During the second week of festivities, the Hudson-Fulton Celebration moved beyond the center stage of Manhattan to the boroughs and the towns along the Hudson River. The program outside of Manhattan followed the Commission's overall scheme for honoring New York's past, particularly through the non-stop, on-river party showcasing the *Half Moon*, the *Clermont*, and modern vessels of all sorts. That said, the history holidays mounted in Ossining, Catskill, and Albany possessed a different flavor and represented a different agenda. In contrast to Manhattan—where organizers broadcast that New York was a modern, world-class city and offered tutorials in citizenship to a large immigrant population—civic leaders in the Hudson Valley were more traditional and less expansive. Hitching their wagon to the recently developed concept of Old Home Week, they hoped that the menu of firework displays, shared meals, and other get-togethers would strengthen individuals' ties to their communities, support local businesses, and encourage pride in local and state history. The divergent approach to parade-making said it all. Unlike Manhattan's message-laden and controlled processions, parades in Tarrytown, Troy, and elsewhere in the Hudson Valley exuded a greater openness. Regiments of club members, firemen, school children, and—most notably—labor unionists marched to stirring tunes played by uniformed bands, through streets ornamented by festoons of electric lights and bunting, to the cheers of thousands of exhilarated spectators. Recalling Hudson's and Fulton's voyages north of Manhattan, and epitomizing the moderate pace and intimate character of American small-town life to which the Metropolis was bidding adieu, these upriver ceremonies provided a fitting conclusion to New York's 1909 history party. ❖

INDUSTRIAL NUMBER

HARPER'S WEEKLY

EDITED BY GEORGE HARVEY

ARTHUR COVEY

October 16 1909   HARPER & BROTHERS, N. Y.   Price 10 Cents

Farmer watching biplane

Published in New York a few days after the conclusion of the Hudson-Fulton Celebration, the cover image on this Harper's Weekly *expresses the dawn of a new day. Air travel as demonstrated by Wright and Curtiss would change the lives of everyday Americans.*

The Party's Over

"For as Venice is the Queen of the Renaissance alone, and splendid and Oriental, so New York is the Queen of the Twentieth Century alone, and splendid in her architectural barbarism of today. . . . New York does possess a beauty of her own, a beauty that is indescribable, that seizes one's sense of imagination and holds one in its grip in a way as does that of no other city."

Mayor George McClellan, Reception at Metropolitan Opera, September 27, 1909

A few days after the conclusion of the Hudson-Fulton Celebration, curious onlookers watched as workmen assembled scaffolding around a fifty-foot-high block of plaster in Longacre (Times) Square. Once the framework was in place, sculptors set to work fashioning a statue of a woman garbed in classical dress standing atop a pedestal. Best known as the Statue of Purity, the angry figure held up a mud-stained shield inscribed "Our City." According to *The New York Times*, "among the slanders and unjust criticism which it aims to put down . . . are the frequent assertions that the city has reached its debt limit and has poor credit, and the aspersions constantly cast upon the integrity and honesty of the municipal authorities." In a mock interview published in the same paper, the statue admitted that her scowl was a bit of an act. From her perch, she could see countless people, including out-of-towners who were often New York's harshest detractors, having the time of their lives. She had even overheard Celebration attendees who had remained in town after the fête admit that they did not want to return to the farm anytime soon. The circumstances surrounding the Statue of Purity were far from sterling —it was erected by a group associated with Tammany Hall, failed to be installed in time for the Celebration as had been planned, and was hardly aesthetically pleasing—yet it starkly represented New York's insecurity about its reputation and its weariness at being criticized for its size, bustle, and sinful ways.[1]

The Statue of Purity
Also known as "The Defeat of Slander" or "Virtue," this marvel wrought in plaster was a temporary art installation during the fall of 1909.

After the last tourist had left Manhattan, the last warship had sailed from New York Harbor, and the last bit of bunting had been packed away, Hudson-Fulton Celebration post-production proceedings got underway. The work began with a full accounting and tidying up of loose ends, but also included a consideration of the city's workings as a whole. The festival revealed a city with resilience even greater than its boosters could have anticipated.

Accounting for every penny accepted and spent was vitally important to Celebration organizers whose progressive approach valued exacting documentation and proof that this was a graft-free affair. They did this by issuing an official report that weighed in at ten and one-half pounds. (The report itself received criticism for being "unnecessarily huge and unnecessarily expensive" in an article titled "Overbalancing Event with Record.") In the chapter outlining the financial system and audited statements, Isaac Seligmann, who served as Treasurer, was recognized for his supreme service. His firm J. & W. Seligmann & Co. even advanced funds to assure cash flow, including $21,000 for disbursements that had not been covered by receipts. In addition, there was approximately $30,000 in unpaid bills. Commissioners hoped that the auction of parade costumes and floats on July 27, 1910, might reduce the deficit. But the stuff of magic had been reduced to scrap, and the low prices bidders paid did little to help. On the bright side, it was estimated that the Celebration netted city hotels, restaurants, and stores sixty million dollars in revenue.[2]

Portrait of Queen Wilhelmina

M. Paul Berthon depicted the monarch wearing Dutch folk dress in 1901. The print was a very popular image in the United States.

There were other issues to be settled. Commission President General Stewart L. Woodford set off for Europe to personally present gold medals to those heads of state who had sent warships to the Celebration. He met with Wilhelmina, Queen of the Netherlands; Wilhelm II, Emperor of Germany; Armand Fallières, President of the French Republic; and Vittorio Emanuele III, King of Italy. His reception by King George of England on June 30, 1910, was the last public act of the Celebration. Meanwhile, United States diplomats gave medals to Porfirio Díaz, President of the United Mexican States, and to José Figueroa Alcorta, President of the Argentine Republic.[3]

The destinies of the *Half Moon* and *Clermont* had not been determined by the end of the Celebration. Assuring the care of the *Half Moon* was particularly important, since it had been a gift from the Netherlands. Some thought that the replica ships should end up in Central Park or in Brooklyn's Prospect Park. After spending the winter in the Brooklyn Navy Yard, the *Half Moon* was given to New York State for display at the Palisades Interstate Park. For some years it was moored near Bear Mountain, but when it became clear that the Park could not properly care for the ship, it was transferred to the city of Cohoes and exhibited in dry dock. Fire destroyed the ship in the 1930s.

Turned down as a gift by the Palisades Interstate Park, the *Clermont* was purchased by the Hudson River Day Line in September 1910 for $1,000. In 1914, the company placed the boat in a lagoon near Kingston Point as part of its pleasure grounds. Two decades later, the Henry Ford Museum of Dearborn, Michigan, purchased the boat for its machinery. The museum took the engine, leaving the rest. A scrap man removed the remains, except for the hull, which remained visible for many years at low tide.[4]

Some legacy projects associated with the Celebration were realized, while others were not, or at least not right away. Among the most important was the creation of the Palisades Interstate Park. It protected a section of the distinctive mountain range near New York City from quarrying and provided city dwellers a place for recreation in a woodland setting. The arch at Stony Point Revolutionary War Battlefield south of Newburgh also enshrined a beautiful and histori-

Celebration postcard
of proposed bridge

cally important landscape. Both were dedicated publicly during the festivities. Promoted as a Celebration memorial project, the Henry Hudson Bridge linking the Bronx and Manhattan was not erected until the 1930s. Talk of constructing a permanent version of the Water Gate, the Celebration's official river landing at 110th Street, never came to fruition. As more visitors came to New York by train and automobile than by boat, building a large-scale dock seemed unwarranted. The Robert Fulton Memorial—a scheme projected for Riverside Park that featured Italian style gardens, promenades, a dock, and a tomb for the remains of the great man and his family—never attracted the three million dollars required for its construction.[5]

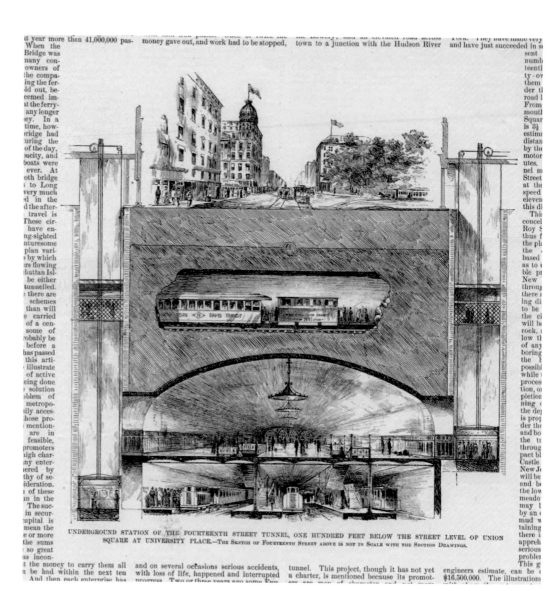

UNDERGROUND STATION OF THE FOURTEENTH STREET TUNNEL, ONE HUNDRED FEET BELOW THE STREET LEVEL OF UNION SQUARE AT UNIVERSITY PLACE.—The Sketch of Fourteenth Street above is not in Scale with the Section Drawings.

The Metropolis fared well in the testing of its infrastructure and its population. For years to come, the subway and elevated lines touted statistics documenting record ridership. Likewise, the New York Edison Company pointed to the strength of the electrical grid and the ability to produce lots of power—not to mention the heights of artistry realized—during nighttime electrical illuminations. The police were credited with keeping visitors and residents safe and not using excessive force in crowd control. More than one commentator noted that crowds attending the event, though numbering in the millions, behaved well and did not riot. Statistics-loving progressives repeatedly noted that crime, death, and suicide rates went down during the two-week event.

On the other hand, the idea of the instructional parade, the historical pageant on the move, did not work. The ill-advised concept was further doomed by poor design, construction, materials, and logistical planning. Wisecracking New Yorkers found humor in the mix-ups, accidents, and errors. The earnestness of the organizers made them an easy target for barbs.

Some critics placed the Hudson-Fulton Celebration squarely in the "bread and circuses" category. For example, father-and-son conservationists John and Poultney Bigelow wrote that the Celebration was a huge waste of money that would have been better spent cleaning up the Hudson River to provide healthy drinking water. John Bigelow failed to see how the Celebration would have a positive impact on working people. In his opinion, they would lose money taking off from work to attend and would lose even more recovering from its excesses.[6] Others believed that the Celebration did not represent the best interests of the laboring class. An editorial in the *New York Call* told workers that:

The bourgeois mind sees in history only individuals performing wonders. . . . 'Successful' New York business men, the dead past clinging to their coat-tails, are quite right in honoring Fulton and forgetting the others [who experimented with steam-powered vehicles before him]. But the intelligent workingman, seeking to understand the facts of industrial development, readily connects their creation of steam navigation, as well as the later steam railroads, to the Industrial Revolution of the latter part of the eighteenth century. Without factories and steam machines turning out enormous masses of products for sale in distant markets, there would have been no need of steam transportation by water and by land, and no impulse for bringing it into existence. Great discoveries and inventions are the products not of individual ingenuity, but of social conditions.[7]

Stereoscope view of the New York Edison Company power plant
The plant, located at East 35th Street, was illuminated during the Celebration.

THE "SWEATING SYSTEM" IN NEW YORK CITY.—[See Page 172.]

1. A Family of Sewing-machine Operators, who Work in a Room 8 Feet long by 8 Feet wide.   2. A "Sweaters" Working and Sleeping Apartment.   3. One of the Larger Sweat-Shops.   4. A Four-year-old Child making a Baby-waist.
the Patterns are at Work.   5. A Family of "Home-workers" making Children's Clothes at 11.30 P.M.; the Rent of this Room is $2.50 a Month.

**Adults and children laboring
in New York sweat shops**

A telling counterpoint to the Celebration was the "Strike of the 20,000" which also began in September 1909. At that time, Clara Lemlich and a few other female garment workers walked off their jobs to protest poor conditions and unfair labor practices. Their action grew to a strike involving thousands of mostly Jewish and Italian women and girls at the Leiserson, Triangle Shirtwaist, and some 500 other factories in Manhattan. Their peaceful processions during the fall and winter were not met with cheers, but with animosity and police beatings. The threat of financial ruin for factory owners forced a settlement in February 1910. But the agreed-upon reforms did not prevent the death of 146 women in the Triangle Shirtwaist Fire a year later, a tragedy caused by illegal working conditions and other inadequacies in safety and building codes.[8]

Encouraging the assimilation of recent immigrants was one of the organizers' goals, but it is hard to ascertain the Celebration's direct impact. In charting the complex process of acculturation at the turn of the twentieth century, historians point to a variety of influences on new immigrants: friends and family who had arrived before; native language newspapers; ethnic, political, labor, and religious organizations; and settlement houses. Among the most powerful acculturators were the New York City public schools and popular culture. In regard to the latter, music, vaudeville acts, dime novels, and advertisements illustrated what looks, words, traits, and beliefs were viewed as typically American, and hence desirable. What is clear is that the patriarchal and patronizing emblem of Father Knickerbocker, a star of the Celebration, faded soon afterward while the "Mother of Exiles," the Statue of Liberty, ascended. Initially, "Liberty Enlightening the World" represented the republican ideals shared by its donor, France, and its recipient, the United States. After the Ellis Island Immigration Station opened nearby in 1892, and a plaque bearing a poem by Emma Lazarus called "The New Colossus"—better known by its line "Give me your tired, your poor"— was mounted inside the statue's base for public display in 1903, it became more closely associated with the welcoming of immigrants to the United States. The statue was abstract enough that recent arrivals could project their own Ameri-

Statue of Liberty illuminated during the Celebration

can dreams upon it, but there were limits to the hospitality it represented. Beginning in 1921, continuing doubts about America's capacity to absorb immigrants resulted in the establishment of quotas that were not favorable to newcomers from eastern and southern Europe.[9]

The Hudson-Fulton Celebration was successful in helping cultural institutions strengthen themselves. Perhaps the Metropolitan Museum took the greatest advantage of the Celebration. The American Industrial Arts exhibition proved that Americans were interested in their own art, and encouraged Robert de Forest and others to go forward with a plan for the American Wing which opened in 1924. The Dutch Masters exhibition attracted the donations of important European paintings to the Metropolitan, but also promoted the idea that American art collectors should share their prized possessions with the public through loans and gifts to art museums. That said, the Celebration did little to engage or raise the profile of individual artists living in New York. The corporate approach to art-making that it represented was harshly criticized.[10] A few years after the Celebration, the ground-breaking Armory Show of 1913 and its shockingly modern art by European and American artists changed the arts environment in New York forever, pushing it past Chicago, Boston, and Philadelphia as

Painting of Naval Parade

Elmer MacRae's Hudson-Fulton Review 1909 *is a rare example of fine art inspired by the Celebration.*

America's most fashion-forward city. New York would develop into an international art capital during the twentieth century.

In regard to transportation, the Celebration introduced air flight to New Yorkers in these first public demonstrations. Glenn Curtiss would win the *New York World* flight contest replicating Fulton's first trip the year after the Celebration.[11] Dirigibles would never be as popular in the United States as they were in Europe or fill the sky as they did in popular images accompanying the Celebration. The twentieth century would be marked by the rise of the subway, the automobile, and, of course, the airplane, as travel by boat and wagon declined. The suburbs grew as advances made commuting to and from the city easier.

The race to build skyscrapers, the hallmark buildings of New York, continued, although a 1916 zoning law restricted their height and shape. The Woolworth Building (1913), the Chrysler Building (1930), the Empire State Building (1931), and Rockefeller Center (1939), among other skyscrapers, added to New York's distinctive and internationally recognized skyline. In 1909, a typical comment in the *Illustrated London News* referred to New York as the "city of dreadful height" in an exhibition review of etchings of urban scenes. By the 1930s, New York City's tremendous verticality would be considered beautiful and sophisticated nationally and even internationally, due in part to its portrayal in Hollywood movies and in the art of Georgia O'Keeffe, Alfred Stieglitz, Charles Sheeler, and Paul Strand.[12]

Obviously, the peaceful meeting of nations in New York did not seriously lessen tensions in Europe. Five years after the Celebration, England, Germany, and other European nations were embroiled in World War I. The devastating 1915 torpedo attack on the *Lusitania*—the British ocean liner Wilbur Wright had buzzed in his airplane as it sailed out of New York Harbor during the Celebration—and the death of more than one hundred American civilians on board encouraged the United States to enter the war in 1917. Mayor George McClellan had reason to rethink the farewell speech he had given during the Celebration, in which he had referred to Kaiser Wilhelm II as "the most potent force for the preservation of European peace."[13] Ominously, the final image in the Celebration's official report was a portrait of the Kaiser.

In 1909, New Yorkers were not simply looking backward to 1609 and 1807, they were also casting a glance toward 2009, the next milestone in the city and state's journey through time. As they praised the deeds of those who had gone on before, they dreamed that twenty-first-century New Yorkers would find their predecessors' actions in 1909 worthy. Commission President Stewart L. Woodford was not alone in evoking New York State one hundred years later, hoping that when children gathered in commemoration "their Half Moon [would] be a full moon of perfect memory and perfect friendship" and that their political leaders would be strong and honest.[14] The 1909 Hudson-Fulton Celebration served as a fulcrum between past accomplishments and aspirations for the future.

Stephen Chalmers, a Scottish-born writer in various genres including science fiction, projected himself and New York one hundred years into the future in a satirical piece he wrote for *The New York Times* in September 1909.[15] Just as Washington Irving had used *A History of New York* to poke fun at his contemporaries in 1809, Chalmers wrote "a future of New York" to do the same. In it, Chalmers assumed the persona of a reporter covering the Hudson-Fulton Quadricentennial for the newspaper, now called the *Universal Times*, in 2009.

Perfectly in keeping with the 1909 organizers' desire to put the whole city on view, Chalmers painted a playful picture of New York's cityscape and transportation options in 2009. In his vision, streets have become dedicated pedestrian walkways because vehicles have taken to the sky. By law, all structures are of a uniform height, allowing dirigible-like aeroliners plenty of room to land and skimmers, another form of craft, to skip along on building roofs. A common mass-transit vehicle is the submarine-aerovessel. Able to travel under water and in the air, riders love it because they don't have to make a transfer. Sky kayaks with beating wings also buzz around Manhattan. Chalmers concocts a bright, Jules Verneian view of the future, not a grim and dehumanizing scenario of the sort imagined by pessimists like H. G. Wells.

Chalmers's image of the 2009 Hudson-Fulton Quadricentennial Celebration is literally out-of-this-world. Representatives from various parts of the solar system participate in a parade of interplanetary aircraft over the Hudson River; some events actually take place on Mars. Assuming the personas of early aviators Wilbur Wright and Glenn Curtiss, residents of Mars and of Hoboken reenact 1909 air flight in an "aeroscat dash" to Chicago and back. The fascination with all things Martian in 1909 could be attributed in large part to astronomer Percival Lowell. In his books *Mars* (1895) and *Mars and Its Canals* (1906), Lowell surmised that the Red Planet must be inhabited by civilized beings because of the seemingly deliberate system of canals on its surface.

As is the case with most science fiction, Chalmers's imaginings were not completely wild and whimsical. Many of his predictions have come to pass. Engineers have harnessed waterfalls and tides to provide electricity. Color images and music are sent and received wirelessly. The Wright Brothers' flying machine, the first submarine, and the horse-drawn trolley (or facsimiles thereof) have been relegated to museums. The language used in 1909 to describe the Hudson-Fulton Celebration does sound quaint to twenty-first-century ears. The era's hot controversy between Robert Peary and Frederick Cook is largely forgot-

Vol. XX | OCTOBER 1909 | No. 79

THE
BURR McINTOSH
MONTHLY

The Half Moon

COPYRIGHT 1909 BY UNDERWOOD & UNDERWOOD N.Y.

24 West 39th St.   BURR PUBLISHING CO.   New York City

Half Moon sailing
into the night

175

AIRSHIPS PASSING WEST POINT—PAINTED BY LOUIS BIEDERMANN. the greatest aerial
spectacle ever witnessed will take place. The celebration commemorates the discovery of the Hudson River
by Henry Hudson in 1609 and its navigation from New York to Albany by Robert Fulton in the first steamboat in 1807. The New York World has offered a $10,000 prize to the aerial navigator who duplicates in
the air the 147-mile journey of Fulton's first steamboat, the *Clermont.*

During the great Hudson-Fulton celebration in New York in September-October, 1909,

Celebration postcard

*This fantastic view of
an air and river parade
captured the event's
optimistic and progres-
sive spirit.*

ten. We do still travel around the city using the subway. And, in an amazing bit
of clairvoyance, Chalmers correctly envisioned that baby strollers would continue to prove an obstacle to pedestrians in 2009!

Sadly, some of his projections did not come true. Chalmers foresaw a place
where the people of the world had united under one government. Battleships
and military parades had become obsolete, because nations settled international disputes at the Hague, the city of peace, rather than on the battlefield. He

also dreamed that a sample of the tuberculin developed by Nobel Prize winner Robert Koch would be enshrined in a museum, the implication being that tuberculosis, a disease rampant in 1909, would be a thing of the past. While a sample of Koch's tuberculin does reside in the collection of the Smithsonian Institution in 2009, the disease has not yet been eradicated.[16]

Both the science fiction writer of 1909 and the historian of 2009 recognize the Hudson-Fulton Celebration as a snapshot of a city, a state, a nation, and a society. The idea of documenting and reflecting upon circumstances every hundred years is not only historically illuminating but also appealing to the collective psyche. And as much as we might be alternately amused, inspired, perplexed, and offended by the progressive mindset of 1909, there is something satisfying in knowing that these civic leaders were convinced that the twentieth century would be New York's century. It would become not only the Metropolis of the western hemisphere, but arguably the greatest city in the world. In documenting the conditions and results of their 1909 history holidays so thoroughly, New Yorkers gave us a lens with which to look back at them and their world, a valuable tool as we consider the viability of the Metropolis of New York, and the whole Hudson Valley, in 2009. ❖

Notes

Introduction

1. Seattle hosted the Alaska-Yukon-Pacific Exposition, Springfield mounted the Abraham Lincoln Centennial, and San Francisco offered up the Portola Festival.

2. "City Dressing in Bunting," *The Evening Post*, September 21, 1909, 1. Courtesy of the New York State Library.

3. Facts about New York City contained in "Metropolis of Hudson and Fulton and Its Century of Enchantment," *New York Herald*, September 26, 1909, magazine section, n.p. Courtesy of the New York State Library.

4. "Peary Found No Trace of Cook at North Pole," *The New York Times*, September 8, 1909, 1. "German Explorers Were Told of Dr. Cook's Achievement by Eskimos Long Before Discoverer Reached Civilization," *New York Herald*, September 16, 1909, 1. "Peary Claims the Pole," *New-York Observer*, September 23, 1909, 391. "Dr. Cook Tells How Last Bit of Land Faded from Sight, Leaving Little Party Alone on the Waste of Ice," *New York Herald*, September 25, 1909, 3. "River Ovation for Peary," *The Evening Post*, October 1, 1909, 1, 12. Courtesy of the New York State Library.

5. "French Airship Explodes, The Republique is Destroyed, Four Officers Killed," *The Evening Post*, September 25, 1909, 1. "Wilbur Wright Sails over the Hudson for Twenty Miles in the Most Spectacular Aeroplane Flight on Record," *New York Herald*, October 5, 1909, 5. Courtesy of the New York State Library.

6. "Mr. Taft at Salt Lake," *New-York Tribune*, September 25, 1909, 1. "Mr. Taft Sounds War Warning," *New York Herald*, October 1, 1909, 7. Courtesy of the New York State Library.

7. "Fusion Conference on Ticket Next Week," *The New York Times*, September 10, 1909, 20. Courtesy of the New York State Library.

8. David Von Drehle, *Triangle: The Fire That Changed America* (New York: Atlantic Monthly Press, 2003), 20–21.

9. "Gen. Woodford Apologizes to Jews," *New-York Tribune*, September 27, 1909, 4. Courtesy of the New York State Library.

10. Edward Hagaman Hall, *The Hudson-Fulton Celebration 1909, The Fourth Annual Report of the Hudson-Fulton Celebration Commission to the Legislature of the State of New York, Transmitted to the Legislature May Twentieth, Nineteen Ten*, 2 vols. (Albany: J. B. Lyon Company, 1910), 1:5–8.

11. *The Encyclopedia of New York City*, ed. Kenneth T. Jackson (New Haven, CT: Yale University Press; New York: New-York Historical Society, 1995), 183. I am grateful to Judy Giuriceo-Lord for sharing information and insights about Ellis Island with me.

12. Hall, *The Hudson-Fulton Celebration 1909*, 1:16–22, 48–57.

A Test of the Modern Metropolis

1. Edward Hagaman Hall, *The Hudson-Fulton Celebration 1909, The Fourth Annual Report of the Hudson-Fulton Celebration Commission to the Legislature of the*
State of New York, Transmitted to the Legislature May Twentieth, Nineteen Ten, 2 vols. (Albany: J. B. Lyon Company, 1910), 1:42. A bit of pre-event publicity reported that mail bags filled with inquiries from all over the nation were arriving daily at Celebration headquarters. "Country Aroused for Fulton Fête," *The New York Times*, September 15, 1909, 7. Courtesy of the New York State Library. Edward Hagaman Hall, *Hudson and Fulton, A Brief History of Henry Hudson and Robert Fulton with Suggestions Designed to Aid the Holding of General Commemorative Exercises and Children's Festivals during the Hudson-Fulton Celebration in 1909* (New York: The Hudson-Fulton Celebration Commission, 1909), 55–57.

2. For example, an estimated two million spectators attended a nighttime parade held on October 12, 1898, in Manhattan. Brooks McNamara, *Day of Jubilee: The Great Age of Public Celebrations in New York, 1788–1909* (New Brunswick, NJ: Rutgers University Press, 1997), 158.

3. "Coney Island Carnival, Fun Resort Closes for Season with Blare and Glare," *New-York Tribune*, September 19, 1909, part II supplement, 6. "Rowdies Rush Revelers, Mardi Gras at Coney Island Closes Amid More Scenes of Rowdyism," *New-York Tribune*, September 19, 1909, 2. Courtesy of the New York State Library.

4. "Police Ready for Fête Emergencies, Mighty Human Machine Has Been Constructed to Insure Public Safety," *New York Herald*, September 22, 1909, 6. "Shifts of 18 Hours for Police Force," *New York Herald*, September 16, 1909, 5. "Hounding Up Panhandlers," *The Evening Post*, September 21, 1909. "Orderly Crowds Skillfully Handled," *The New York Times*, September 29, 1909, 2. Courtesy of the New York State Library.

5. "On the Watch for Crooks," *The New York Times*, September 4, 1909, 16. "Detective Robbed on Train, Pickpocket Caught, Says He Came Here to Work H-F Crowds," *The New York Times*, September 21, 1909, 3. "To Put Embargo on Criminals For Fête," *New York Herald*, September 18, 1909, 5. "No Mercy for Pickpockets," *The New York Times*, September 25, 1909, 3. "Hounding Up Panhandlers," *The Evening Post*, September 21, 1909, 4. Courtesy of the New York State Library.

6. Hall, *The Hudson-Fulton Celebration 1909*, 1:21. "Crowd Little Trouble," *New-York Tribune*, October 3, 1909, 2. "Never before had the police been disposed to act so sanely in the continual and rather unpleasant struggle with thoughtless sightseers." "Echoes of the Naval Parade," *The Evening Post*, September 27, 1909, 4. "Praises Our Police, Kaiser's Representative at the Hudson-Fulton Jubilee Says They Are Efficient," *The New York Times*, December 22, 1909, 20. "Good Work by the Police," *The Evening Post*, September 29, 1909, 3. Courtesy of the New York State Library.

7. *The Hudson-Fulton Celebration Information Booklet* (New York: Public Health and Convenience Committee of the Hudson-Fulton Celebration Commission, 1909), 4–5, 6–7, 10.

8. *The Hudson-Fulton Celebration Information Booklet*, 12–16. Advertisements for "Furnished Rooms of the Better Class," *The New York Times*, September 15, 1909, 17. "Notable Guests at Hotel," *The New York Times*, September 22, 1909, 3. "Hotel is Gay with Guests," *The New York Times*, September 29, 1909, 3. "Moors Come with Slaves," *The New York Times*, September 29, 1909, 3. "Hotel Stands Filled," *The New*

York Times, October 1, 1909, 2. "Dripping Crowds Crane Their Necks," *New York Herald*, September 28, 1909. 6. "The Celebration's Income and Cost," *The Evening Post*, October 9, 1909, supplement 1. "State Hotel Men Hold Their Dinner," *The New York Times*, December 3, 1909, 6. "Fulton Applicants Swamp the Hotels," *The New York Times*, September 14, 1909, 3. Courtesy of the New York State Library.

9. "Coastwise Liners Show Big Traffic, Freight and Passenger Increases Point to a Record-Breaking Season for all Lines," *The New York Times*, August 23, 1909, 14. "Railroads Taxed by Fulton Crowd Rush," *The New York Times*, September 25, 1909, 3. "Many Visitors to East," *The New York Times*, September 26, 1909, 11. Advertisement for The Automobile Exchange, *The New York Times*, September 26, 1909, XX8. Courtesy of the New York State Library.

10. "Records Smashed on Subway and 'L'," *New York Herald*, October 4, 1909, 5. "Records Made Here in Handling Crowds," *The New York Times*, October 4, 1909, 3. "Railroad Courtesies for Visiting Tars," *The New York Times*, September 14, 1909, 3. "4,000,000 Jam All Lines of Traffic," *New York Herald*, September 26, 1909, first section, n.p. "Profits from A Celebration," *The Evening Post*, October 9, 1909, financial section 3. "Quote American to Disapprove Hearst, Tammany Cites Editor on Rise in Inter-Met," *The New York Times*, October 19, 1909, 2. Courtesy of the New York State Library.

11. "Vast Crowd for Pageant," *The Evening Post*, September 28, 1909, 1–2. "Plight of Riverside Park," *The Evening Post*, September 27, 1909, 3. "Street Cleaners Gave Aid," *The Evening Post*, October 5, 1909, 3. Courtesy of the New York State Library.

12. "Keeping Down Price of Carnival Seats," *The New York Times*, September 17, 1909, 4. "Revokes Permits for Fulton Stands," *The New York Times*, September 19, 1909, 20. "Smith Tears Down Patriots' Stands," *The New York Times*, September 22, 1909, 4. "Fulton Stand Row Worries Patriots," *The New York Times*, September 22, 1909, 4. Courtesy of the New York State Library.

13. Barbara Kimmelman, "Design and Construction of the IRT: Electrical Engineering." Survey Number Historical American Engineering Record, NY-122, National Park Service, 283–363. http://www.nycsubway.org/articles/haer-design-electrical.html (accessed July 7, 2007).

14. Advertisement for New York Edison Company, *The New York Times*, September 3, 1909, 7. Advertisement for New York Edison Company, *The New York Times*, September 15, 1909, 4. Advertisement for New York Edison Company, *The New York Times*, August 18, 1909, 4. "Wonders in Lighting," *The New York Times*, July 15, 1909, 6. "Turn Night into Day for Hudson Festival," *The New York Times*, September 3, 1909, 18. Advertisement for New York Edison Company, *The New York Times*, October 3, 1909, 7. In this testing of the power grid, capacity was never reached, partially due to homeowners turning off their light fixtures when they went out to see nighttime festivities. Engineers and men working at power plants watched the load carefully. "Record Light Display," *The Evening Post*, October 4, 1909, 12. "What Hudson-Fulton Illuminations Mean to the Future," *The New York Times*, October 1, 1909, SM1. "Mars and Hudson-Fulton," *The New York Times*, September 5, 1909, 8. Courtesy of the New York State Library.

15. "World's Tallest Building in Blaze of Electricity," *New York Herald*, September 24, 1909, 5. Courtesy of the New York State Library. Belle Greene to Bernard Berenson, September 27, 1909 in Jean Strouse, *Morgan: American Financier* (New York: Random House, 1999), 611.

16. Hall, *The Hudson-Fulton Celebration 1909*, 1:122. "Play Tricks on Night," *New-York Tribune*, September 25, 1909, 4. "Fulton's Old Ship in 'Steam Fireworks,'" *New York Herald*, September 24, 1909, 6. Two locomotives provided the steam for the *Clermont* steamship effect. "Record Light Display," *The Evening Post*, October 4, 1909, 12. Courtesy of the New York State Library.

17. "Flashes of Fun; Flights of Fancy," *New York Herald*, September 26, 1909, first section, n.p. "Sidelights on the Show," *The New York Times*, September 28, 1909, 5. "Mailed Letter in Firebox," *The New York Times*, October 7, 1909, 8. "Country Cousin is Here," *The Evening Post*, September 23, 1909, 1. "Dripping Crowds Crane Their Necks," *New York Herald*, September 28, 1909, 6. "Back After 47 Years; He Finds a Magic City," *New York Herald*, September 27, 1909, 9. "Seeing New York After 47 Years," *The New York Times*, September 27, 1909, 3. Courtesy of the New York State Library.

18. "A Test of New York," *The Evening Post*, September 27, 1909, 6. Courtesy of the New York State Library.

The Quandary of New York History

1. Irving continuously revised subsequent editions of *A History of New York* (1809) in an effort to keep the satire's references current, to reflect changes in his political opinions and those of the American public, and to soften or eliminate certain barbs. Irving wrote a half-hearted "Author's Apology" as a preface to the author's revised edition published by G. P. Putnam in 1848. While acknowledging the work's sting, he also claimed that the world would not have known about New York's early Dutch customs, nor would have enjoyed them as "convivial currency," if it had not been for Knickerbocker's *History*. Washington Irving, *A History of New York*, ed. Michael L. Black and Nancy B. Black (Boston: Twayne Publishers, 1984), li–lii, 3–5.

2. Knickerbocker's *History* was well received by European literati. Samuel Taylor Coleridge was reported to have stayed up most of the night reading a copy, while Sir Walter Scott read it aloud to his wife and guests and then reported "our sides have been absolutely sore with laughing." Irving, *A History of New York*, xl. Stanley T. Williams and Mary Allen Edge, *A Bibliography of the Writings of Washington Irving, A Check List* (1936; reprint, New York: Burt Franklin, 1970), 61–69.

3. "The Immortal Diedrich," *The Evening Post*, October 2, 1909, 4. Courtesy of the New York State Library. Edward Hagaman Hall, *The Hudson-Fulton Celebration 1909, The Fourth Annual Report of the Hudson-Fulton Celebration Commission to the Legislature of the State of New York, Transmitted to the Legislature May Twentieth, Nineteen Ten*, 2 vols. (Albany: J. B. Lyon Company, 1910), 1:337, 1038, 6–7.

Although the standard, 10-volume *The History of the State of New York* edited by Alexander C. Flick and Dixon Ryan Fox would not be published by Columbia University until 1933–1937, historians had been addressing New York's past in a serious way since the mid-nineteenth century. Two of these historian-archivists laid the groundwork for the kind of document-based, analytical approach historians employ today. John Romeyn Brodhead gathered research materials in European repositories relating to New York's early history in 1841, during a diplomatic mission to the Netherlands. Although he eventually authored the multi-volume *History of the State of New York* (1853–1871), it fell to E. B. O'Callaghan to translate and publish the transcripts Brodhead had amassed. O'Callaghan came to the historian-archivist's profession in a circuitous way. Born in County Cork and schooled in Paris, this medical doctor migrated to Quebec where he was elected to the Lower Assembly. Involved in a failed political insurrection, he fled to Albany, New York, where he adopted the cause of the Hudson Valley's tenant farmers, publishing the anti-rent newspaper *Northern Light* and learning old Dutch in order to understand manorial claims. His books on New York included *History of New Netherland* (1846) and the four-volume *Documentary History of New York* (1849–1851). *Appleton's Cyclopedia of American Biography*, ed. James Grant Wilson and John Riske, 6 vols. (New York: D. Appleton and Company, 1887), 1:382–3; *Appleton's Cyclopedia*, 4:551. Joseph H. Meany, Jr., "New York: The State of History," essay compiled in 1994 and revised in 2001. http://www.nysm.nysed.gov/services/meanydoc.html (accessed April 10, 2007).

Other writers took a more popular approach to chronicling New York's past, reflective of New York City's premier position as the center of commercial publishing in the United States. Newspaper editor and wood engraver Benson Lossing wrote and illustrated numerous books and articles on the topic including *The Hudson, From the Wilderness to the Sea* (1866). His other works that focused partially or solely on New York history included *Pictorial Field-Book of the Revolution* issued serially (1850–1852), *The Life and Times of Philip Schuyler* (1872–1873), *History of New York City* (1884), *Two Spies: Nathan Hale and John André* (1886), and *The Empire State, a Compendious History of the Commonwealth of New York* (1887). Martha J. Lamb authored *History of the City of New York* (1877–1880) and *Homes of America* (1879). The latter featured many houses located in New York. *Appleton's*, 4:331. *Appleton's*, 3:599–600. http://asteria.fivecolleges.edu/findaids/sophiasmith/mnsss39_bioghist.html (accessed April 15, 2007).

4. "There is yet no monumental history of the State of New York, and it must be confessed that New York is far from the position of historical eminence which she would hold, in the estimation of her own people but also of the nation at large, if there were a more popular familiarity with her annals." Hall, *The Hudson-Fulton Celebration 1909*, 1:7. Circa 1909, Beard and other maverick historians were developing a new approach to writing American history. They placed high value on the close study of the historical record and unbiased analysis over the passionate promulgation of political and cultural agendas, thus helping to forge practices accepted as the professional standard today. For information about the conflict between the New York State Historian, the State Library of New York, and the State Education Department, see Bruce W. Dearstyne, "Archival Politics in New York State, 1892–1915," *New York History* 66 (April 1985): 164–184. Hall, *The Hudson-Fulton Celebration 1909*, 1:362.

5. "And the sage Oloffe dreamed a dream . . . and he hastened and climbed up to the top of one of the tallest trees, and saw that the smoke . . . assumed a variety of marvelous forms, where in dim obscurity he saw shadowed out palaces and domes and lofty spires, all of which lasted but a moment, and then faded away, until the whole rolled off, and nothing but the green woods were left." Irving, *A History of New York*, 76–77.

6. For example, the first history of New York, penned by New Englander William Smith in 1757 but published posthumously in 1814, did not reference any Dutch records. The New Netherland Project established by the New York State Library and Holland Society of New York continues the work of translating early New York records in Dutch into English.

7. William Dunlap, *A History of New York, For Schools*, 2 vols. (New York: Collins, Keese, & Co., 1837), 2:1–17. The artist, playwright, art critic, and historian William Dunlap (1766–1839) is best known for his *History of the Rise and Progress of the Art of Design in the United States* (1834) where his favoritism for New York is apparent. He also authored *New Netherlands* (1840). For more information about his life, see *Appleton's*, 2:259.

8. For information about the role New England played in the development of American identity, see Sarah Burns, *Pastoral Inventions: Rural Life in Nineteenth-Century American Art and Culture* (Philadelphia: Temple University Press, 1989); Joseph A. Conforti, *Imagining New England: Explorations of Regional Identity from the Pilgrims to the Mid-Twentieth Century* (Chapel Hill: University of North Carolina Press, 2001); and *Picturing Old New England: Image and Memory*, ed. William H. Truettner and Roger B. Stein (New Haven: Yale University Press, 1999). "History of the Hudson," *New-York Tribune*, September 25, 1909, unpaginated supplement. Courtesy of the New York State Library. A New York State Education Department booklet also stressed that the Pilgrims, after receiving a warm welcome in Holland, sailed in 1619 in hopes of landing in the Hudson Valley, but found themselves in Massachusetts due to foul weather or deceit. Harlan Hoyt Horner, *Hudson-Fulton Celebration, September 25 to October 9, 1909* (Albany, NY: New York State Education Department, 1909), 4. In hopes of putting a better spin on the purchase of Manhattan, the official parade commentary asserted that twenty-four dollars paid for Manhattan was a "moderate" price. *Historical Pageant, Hudson-Fulton Celebration, September 25 to October 9, 1909* (New York: Printed for the Hudson-Fulton Celebration Commission by Redfield Brothers, 1909), 23.

9. The historical character of Father Knickerbocker dates back to 1898 at least, when he appeared on the cover of *The City History Club Annual Report* leading children of various nationalities in dance. William Rhodes, "Colonial Revival and the Americanization of Immigrants," in *The Colonial Revival in America*, ed. Alan Axelrod (New York: W. W. Norton & Company, 1985), 343.

10. Adam W. Sweeting, *Reading Houses and Building Books: Andrew Jackson Downing and the Architecture of Popular Antebellum Literature, 1835–1855* (Hanover, NH: University Press of New England, 1996), 65–66.

11. Hall, *The Hudson-Fulton Celebration 1909*, 1:7.

Hudson's Valor, Fulton's Genius

1. In some articles, Fulton's Scotch-Irish ancestry was noted. His father came from Kilkenny, Ireland. In the History Parade, Fulton-related floats were accompanied by the Irish-American Athletic Club, the Scotch Color Guard, and United Scotch Societies. Edward Hagaman Hall, *The Hudson-Fulton Celebration 1909, The Fourth Annual Report of the Hudson-Fulton Celebration Commission to the Legislature of the State of New York, Transmitted to the Legislature May Twentieth, Nineteen Ten*, 2 vols. (Albany: J. B. Lyon Company, 1910), 1:292.

2. Donald S. Johnson, *Charting the Sea of Darkness: The Four Voyages of Henry Hudson* (Camden, ME: International Marine, 1993), 74–81.

3. Milton W. Hamilton, *Henry Hudson and the Dutch in New York* (Albany, NY: University of the State of New York 1959), 28. Johnson, *Charting the Sea*, 130–132, 89–127. Donald Johnson includes transcripts of Juet's and Hudson's entries for the 1609 trip arranged by day for ease in comparison.

4. Hall, *The Hudson-Fulton Celebration 1909*, 1:422, 425.

5. Hall, *The Hudson-Fulton Celebration 1909*, 1:419, 422, 423, 425.

6. *The Master, Mate & Pilot* 2 (October 1909): 12. Hall, *The Hudson-Fulton Celebration 1909*, 1:421–422. Joseph I. C. Clarke and Elbert Hubbard, *Manhattan and Henry Hudson* (East Aurora, NY: Roycroft Press, 1910), 42.

7. Washington Irving, *A History of New York*, ed. Michael L. Black and Nancy B. Black (Boston: Twayne Publishers, 1984), 52–53.

8. Francis J. Molson, "The Boy Inventor in American Series Fiction, 1900–1930," *Journal of Popular Fiction* 28 (1994): 31–48. Reprinted in http://xroads.virginia.edu/~public/temp1/temp2/tech_image/article.html (accessed August 30, 2007). *New-York Tribune*, September 25, 1909, "Old New York and New" section, n.p. Courtesy of the New York State Library. The most famous boy inventor in literature, Tom Swift, did not appear until 1910.

9. Cynthia Owen Philip, *Robert Fulton: A Biography* (New York: Franklin Watts, 1985), 45–46. The other standard biographies on Fulton are H. W. Dickinson, *Robert Fulton: Engineer and Artist, His Life and Works* (London: John Lane, 1913) and Kirkpatrick Sale, *The Fire of His Genius: Robert Fulton and the American Dream* (New York: The Free Press, 1981).

10. Philip, 260–261.

11. Philip, 47, 316–317, 343–344. Fulton pursued a long-term "trinity marriage" with Joel and Ruth Barlow. Philip, 102–104 and Sale, 78–79.

12. Philip, 155–156.

13. "Hudson Celebration Plans Made Early," *The New York Times*, June 7, 1907, 6. "Celebrating a Monopoly," *The New York Times* September 28, 1907, 8. Courtesy of the New York State Library.

14. "Robert Fulton's Shade," *New-York Tribune*, October 4, 1909, 5. Courtesy of the New York State Library. Alice Crary Sutcliffe, "Robert Fulton, the Man: A Talk Illustrated with Lantern Slides," typescript, 1909–1910. Collection of Clermont State Historic Site, Germantown, NY. I am grateful to Bruce Naramore for sharing this document with me.

Thomas P. Tuite, "Robert Fulton," *The Irish-American*, September 18, 1909, 1, 3. Courtesy of the New York State Library.

15. As part of the Celebration festivities, eight bronze copies of Jean Antoine Houdon's bust of Fulton were cast and distributed to various repositories. "Honoring Great Inventor," *New-York Observer*, September 30, 1909, 423. Courtesy of the New York State Library. Hall, *The Hudson-Fulton Celebration, 1909*, 1: 717. *The New-York Observer*, a Christian weekly, covered Hudson-Fulton Celebration news and themes in such articles as the sermon-like "The Significance of Hudson and Fulton," *New-York Observer*, September 30, 1909, 425–426. Courtesy of the New York State Library. Edward Hagaman Hall, *Hudson and Fulton, A Brief History of Henry Hudson and Robert Fulton with Suggestions Designed To Aid the Holding of General Commemorative Exercises and Children's Festivals During the Hudson-Fulton Celebration in 1909* (New York: The Hudson-Fulton Celebration Commission, 1909), 67–71.

16. Hall, *The Hudson-Fulton Celebration 1909*, 1:250.

17. "Race Suicide," *The New York Times*, September 25, 1905, 6. "Favors Race Suicide," *The New York Times*, January 8, 1906, 2. Courtesy of the New York State Library. Linda Gordon, *The Moral Property of Women: A History of Birth Control Politics in America* (Urbana and Chicago, University of Illinois Press, 2002), 83–91.

18. Hall, *The Hudson-Fulton Celebration 1909*, 2:1083. "The Hudson-Fulton Celebration, A Letter from Chief Daniel Boone to S. D. B.," unidentified clipping, probably from *Women's Home Companion*, 1909. Private collection.

Parades & Politics

1. "2,000,000 View Land Pageant," *The New York Times*, September 29, 1909, 1. "Kaiser's Son May Come Here," *The New York Times*, February 11, 1909, 1. "May Parade in Rain Today," *The New York Times*, September 28, 1909, 1. Courtesy of the New York State Library.

2. "Country Aroused for Fulton Fête," *The New York Times*, September 5, 1909, 7. Courtesy of the New York State Library. When describing the History Parade in his news dispatch dated September 28, Rudolph Diamant noted that "rich and poor [were] part of the same parade." Lincoln Diamant, *Hoopla on the Hudson: An Intimate View of New York's Great Celebration of 1909* (Fleischmanns, NY: Purple Mountain Press, 2003), 93. "2,000,000 View Land Pageant," *The New York Times*, September 29, 1909, 1. Courtesy of the New York State Library.

3. Brooks McNamara, *Day of Jubilee: The Great Age of Public Celebrations in New York, 1788–1909* (New Brunswick, NJ: Rutgers University Press, 1997), 18–20, 159–60. Edward Hagaman Hall, *The Hudson-Fulton Celebration 1909, The Fourth Annual Report of the Hudson-Fulton Celebration Commission to the Legislature of the State of New York, Transmitted to the Legislature May Twentieth, Nineteen Ten*, 2 vols. (Albany: J. B. Lyon Company, 1910), 1:287.

4. Gustav Stickley, "The People and the Pageant," *The Craftsman* 17 (November 1909): 223–7, 223. http://digicoll.library.wisc.edu (accessed Sept. 3, 2007).

5. Obituary of Bror Anders Wikstrom, *American Art Annual* 7 (1909–10): 82. Samuel V. Hoffman, President of the New-York Historical Society, chaired the Celebration's historical committee. Hall, *The Hudson-Fulton Celebration 1909*, 1:282. "Artist Dies at Easel," *The New York Times*, April 28, 1909, 1. Obituary of James Tauber, *The New York Times*, February 20, 1912, 11. Courtesy of the New York State Library.

6. Hall, *The Hudson-Fulton Celebration 1909*, 1:284–5. "Admirals Rival for Hudson Honors," *The New York Times*, September 6, 1909, 6. Courtesy of the New York State Library.

7. *Historical Pageant, Hudson-Fulton Celebration, September 25 to October 9, 1909* (New York: Printed for the Hudson-Fulton Celebration Commission by Redfield Brothers Inc.), 1909, 8.

8. Hall, *The Hudson-Fulton Celebration 1909*, 1:471.

9. *Historical Pageant*, 56.

10. Hall, *The Hudson-Fulton Celebration 1909*, 1:287.

11. Hall, *The Hudson-Fulton Celebration 1909*, 1:287.

12. Hall, *The Hudson-Fulton Celebration 1909*, 1:302.

13. "The Hudson-Fulton Celebration," *New York Press*, September 19, 1909, section 2, 1. "Land Pageants to Set a Mark for World," *New York Herald*, September 21, 1909, 6. Courtesy of the New York State Library. Rudolph Diamant, news dispatch dated September 28, 1909 in Lincoln Diamant, *Hoopla on the Hudson: An Intimate View of New York's Great 1909 Hudson-Fulton Celebration* (Fleischmanns, NY: Purple Mountain Press, 2003), 91.

14. "Latter Day Pageants," *The Evening Post*, September 29, 1909, 8. Courtesy of the New York State Library. Stickley, "The People and the Pageant," 223, 224. Untitled [From the Artistic Point of View], *The Evening Post*, October 5, 1909, 6. Courtesy of the New York State Library.

15. Hall, *The Hudson-Fulton Celebration 1909*, 1:287–8.

16. Hall, *The Hudson-Fulton Celebration 1909*, 1:286.

17. "Hudson-Fulton Parade," *The New York Times*, May 2, 1909, 6. Courtesy of the New York State Library. Stickley, "The People and the Pageant," 223. "Latter Day Pageants," *The Evening Post*, September 29, 1909, 8. "Echoes of the 'Hudson Show'," *The Evening Post*, September 29, 1909, 14. Courtesy of the New York State Library.

18. "2,000,000 View Land Pageant," *The New York Times*, September 29, 1909, 1. "Multitude Applauds 54 Historical Floats; Reviewed by Governor and Vice President," *New York Herald*, September 29, 1909, 5. Courtesy of the New York State Library. Stickley, "The People and the Pageant," 224, 223. Hall, *The Hudson-Fulton Celebration 1909*, 1:288.

19. Gustav Kobbé, *Hudson-Fulton Celebration: 1909* (New York: Society of Iconophiles, 1910), 32–33. Marie Jastrow, *Looking Back: The American Dream Through Immigrant Eyes* (New York: W. W. Norton & Co., 1986), 120–121.

20. Police estimated that a crowd of 1.2 million "found an inspiring historical lesson." "Multitude Applauds 54 Historical Floats; Reviewed by Governor and Vice President," *New York Herald*, September 29, 1909, 5. "Historical Pageant Gorgeous Spectacle," *New-York Tribune*, September 29, 1909, 1. Courtesy of the New York State Library. A typical postcard reads "Having beautiful weather in New York. Parade yester-

day was fine. Splendid seats, but the crowds! I shall never forget." Private collection. The artist John Sloan described the parade in his diary. "We went . . . to see the 'Grand Pageant.' . . . The crowds were awe inspiring. The floats just big old fashioned toys on a large scale, expensive I suppose." *John Sloan's New York Scene: From the Diaries, Notes and Correspondence 1906–1913*, ed. Bruce St. John (New York, Harper & Row, 1965), 336-337.

21. *The Master, Mate & Pilot* 2 (October 1909): 5, 8. Hall, *The Hudson-Fulton Celebration 1909*, 1:361–3.

22. Hall, *The Hudson-Fulton Celebration 1909*, 1:372.

23. *The Master, Mate & Pilot*, 8.

24. http://www.ulib.iupui.edu/kade/adams/chap5.html (accessed August 23, 2007).

25. "Night Carnival Parade Stirs Multitude to Wild Enthusiasm," *New York Herald*, October 3, 1909, 5. Untitled [From the Artistic Point of View], *The Evening Post*, October 5, 1909, 6. Courtesy of the New York State Library.

26. "Carnival Worries Police," *The Evening Post*, September 22, 1909, 3. "Coney Island Carnival, Fun Resort Closes for Season with Blare and Glare," *New-York Tribune*, September 19, 1909, part II supplement, 6. "Rowdies Rush Revelers, Mardi Gras at Coney Island Closes Amid More Scenes of Rowdyism," *New-York Tribune*, September 19, 1909, 2. Untitled [From the Artistic Point of View], *The Evening Post*, October 5, 1909, 6. Courtesy of the New York State Library. Stickley, "The People and the Pageant," 224.

27. "A Plea for Military Music," *The Evening Post*, October 4, 1909, 6. "History Pageant Criticised [*sic*]," *The Evening Post*, October 4, 1909, 7. Courtesy of the New York State Library.

The Littlest Knickerbockers on Parade

1. Harlan Hoyt Horner, *Hudson-Fulton Celebration, September 25 to October 9, 1909* (Albany: New York State Education Department, 1909), 5. "An Army of 700,000 School Children," *The New York Times*, September 19, 1909, SM2. Courtesy of the New York State Library. Other instructional pamphlets designed to guide Education Day and Children's Day Celebrations included: Edward Hagaman Hall, *Hudson and Fulton, A Brief History of Henry Hudson and Robert Fulton with Suggestions Designed To Aid the Holding of General Commemorative Exercises and Children's Festivals During the Hudson-Fulton Celebration in 1909* (New York: The Hudson-Fulton Celebration Commission, 1909) and Norbert John Melville, *Hudson-Fulton Pageant of Dramatizations: A Typical Pageant of United States History* (New York: Hinds, Noble & Eldredge, 1909).

2. Statewide, principals awarded prizes provided by the Hudson-Fulton Commission for the best history-related essays written by a boy and by a girl. "Aeroplanes Fly, Dirigibles Fail, In City's Celebration," *New York Press*, September 30, 1909, 1–2, 2. "Schools Participate," *New York Call*, September 10, 1909, 7. Courtesy of the New York State Library. Hall, *Hudson and Fulton*, 12.

3. "Children to Share in Hudson Festival," *The New York Times*, August 8, 1909, 16. Courtesy of the New York State Library.

4. William Rhodes, "Colonial Revival and the Americanization of Immigrants," in *The Colonial Revival in America.* ed. Alan Axelrod (New York: W. W. Norton & Company, 1985), 342–345.

5. "400,000 Children Take Part in Celebration Exercises," *New York Press*, October 3, 1909, 2. Courtesy of the New York State Library.

6. "25,000 Pupils Parading," *The Evening Post*, October 2, 1909, 2. "500,000 Children Sing in the Parks," *New York Herald*, October 3, 1909, first section, 5. Over 400,000 hats and flags were purchased for young participants. "Children Training for Hudson Pageant," *The New York Times*, September 8, 1909, 14. Courtesy of the New York State Library.

7. "Children's Day on Staten Island," *New-York Tribune*, October 2, 1909, 5. Courtesy of the New York State Library. Edward Hagaman Hall, *The Hudson-Fulton Celebration 1909, The Fourth Annual Report of the Hudson-Fulton Celebration Commission to the Legislature of the State of New York, Transmitted to the Legislature May Twentieth, Nineteen Ten*, 2 vols. (Albany: J. B. Lyon Company, 1910) 1:507, 510, 507–508. "Day of School Children," *The Sun*, October 3, 1909, 3. Courtesy of the New York State Library.

8. "400,000 Children Take Part in Celebration Exercises," *New York Press*, October 3, 1909, 2. Courtesy of the New York State Library. Hall, *The Hudson-Fulton Celebration 1909*, 1:506–507. "Children Have a Day," *New-York Tribune*, October 3, 1909, 3. Courtesy of the New York State Library. Hall, *Hudson and Fulton*, 71. "When School Turns Into the Land of 1,000 Dances," *The New York Times*, June 20, 2006, B1, B6.

9. Kathleen Eagen Johnson, "From Frans Hals to Windmills: The Arts and Crafts Fascination with the Culture of the Low Countries," in *Substance of Style: Perspectives on the American Arts and Crafts Movement*, ed. Bert Denker (Winterthur, DE: Henry Francis du Pont Winterthur Museum, 1996), 50–51, 67.

10. "200,000 in Children's Fête," *The New York Times*, July 17, 1909, 2. Courtesy of the New York State Library. Rhodes, 342–343. This suggestion aped the organization of the History of New York and Carnival Parades, with their culminating floats featuring Father Knickerbocker and Uncle Sam respectively.

11. "Aeroplanes Fly, Dirigibles Fail, In City's Celebration," *New York Press*, September 30, 1909, 1–2. Courtesy of the New York State Library. Melville, 5–6. "25,000 Pupils Parading," *The Evening Post*, October 2, 1909, 2. Courtesy of the New York State Library.

12. "School Children Portray the City's History," *New York Herald*, September 30. 1909, 6. Courtesy of the New York State Library.

13. "Comedy Written by Nun on Hudson-Fulton Theme," *The New York Press*, September 29, 1909, 2. Courtesy of the New York State Library.

14. "Hudson and The Children," *The Evening Post*, September 25, 1909, 4. "400,000 Children Take Part in Celebration Exercises," *New York Press*, October 3, 1909, 2. Courtesy of the New York State Library.

15. Israel Zangwill, *The Melting-Pot, A Drama in Four Acts* (New York: Macmillan, 1919), 184.

16. Howard Zinn, *A People's History of the United States, 1492–Present* (1980; reprint, New York: Perennial Classics, 2003), 350. "Sunday Schools That Teach Children Anarchy," *The New York Times*, May 8, 1910, SM8. Courtesy of the New York State Library.

17. "Hughes and Cook Meet at Dinner," *The New York Times*, September 29, 1909, 3. "Children Have a Day," *New York Tribune*, October 3, 1909, 3. Courtesy of the New York State Library.

Jump-Starting New York's Arts & Culture

1. For discussion and relative ranking of art museums in Boston, Philadelphia, and New York at the turn of the twentieth century, see Nathaniel Burt, *Palaces for the People: A Social History of the American Art Museum* (Boston: Little, Brown & Company, 1977), 86–150.

2. Edward Hagaman Hall, *The Hudson-Fulton Celebration 1909, The Fourth Annual Report of the Hudson-Fulton Celebration Commission to the Legislature of the State of New York, Transmitted to the Legislature May Twentieth, Nineteen Ten*, 2 vols. (Albany: J. B. Lyon Company, 1910), 1:177.

3. Hall, *The Hudson-Fulton Celebration 1909*, 1:5–6.

4. Hall, *The Hudson-Fulton Celebration 1909*, 1:177.

5. Hall, *The Hudson-Fulton Celebration 1909*, 1:175.

6. Alanson Skinner, "The Indians of Manhattan Island and Vicinity," *American Museum Journal* 9 (September 1909): 143–193. Hall, *The Hudson-Fulton Celebration 1909*, 1:183–184. "Old N.Y. Indians Revived," *The Evening Post*, September 27, 1909, 4. Courtesy of the New York State Library. *Official Program, Hudson-Fulton Celebration* (New York: Printed for the Hudson-Fulton Celebration Commission by Redfield Brothers, 1909), 28. "A Great Historical Exposition," *The New York Times*, September 18, 1909, 8. Courtesy of the New York State Library. Hall, *The Hudson-Fulton Celebration 1909*, 1:191–192.

7. "New York Art For 300 Years," *The New York Times*, July 28, 1909, 3. Courtesy of the New York State Library. Hall, *The Hudson-Fulton Celebration 1909*, 1:188, 190, 188–189, 184–185, 189. R. W. G. Vail, *Knickerbocker Birthday: A Sesqui-Centennial History of the New-York Historical Society, 1804–1954* (New York: New-York Historical Society, 1954), 427. The official report noted that the New-York Historical Society served the Celebration in other ways. Researchers mined the Society's collections when planning the program of events. It also became the repository for the official papers of the Celebration and for the antique furnishings used in Henry Hudson's cabin on the *Half Moon*, a gift from the government of the Netherlands. Hall, *The Hudson-Fulton Celebration 1909*, 1:102, 104, 241.

8. Hall, *The Hudson-Fulton Celebration 1909*, 1:174. "News and Notes," *The New York Times*, December 20, 1908, X6. Courtesy of the New York State Library. J. P. Morgan had worked with Clarke at the Victoria & Albert (South Kensington) Museum when they had headed up the board of trustees and staff. Morgan recruited Clarke to come to the Metropolitan Museum. All the members of the Celebration's art exhibition subcommittee had a connection to the Metropolitan Museum of Art: board of trustees' president and major donor J. P. Morgan, board secretary Robert de Forest, major donor George Hearn, museum director Sir Caspar Purdon Clarke, and curator Edward Robinson.

9. Hall, *The Hudson-Fulton Celebration 1909*, 1:178–179. While not all of these "Old Master" attributions have stood the test of time, many have and today are anchors in American museums. For more information about the Hudson-Fulton Celebration exhibition see Esmée Quodbach, "The Age of Rembrandt: Dutch Paintings in The Metropolitan Museum of Art." *Metropolitan Museum of Art Bulletin* (Summer 2007); reprint, New Haven, Yale University, 2007, 27–30.

10. "Museum of Art Buys Blackborne Laces," *The New York Times*, May 11, 1909, 6. "Great American Art Collectors Contribute to the Hudson-Fulton Exhibition," *New-York Tribune*, September 19, 1909, section 3, 6. Courtesy of the New York State Library. Natalie Curtis, "The Hudson-Fulton Memorial Art Exhibit in New York," *The Craftsman* 17 (November 1909): 124–141, 124. http://digicoll.library.wisc.edu (accessed April 14, 2008). International reviews of the exhibition included Max J. Friedländer, "Die Ausstellung Holländischer Bilder im Metropolitan Museum zu New York 1909," *Repertorium für Kunstwissenschaft* 33 (1910): 95–99 and Joseph Breck, "Hollandsche kunst op de Hudson-Fulton tentoonstelling te New York," *Onze Kunst* 17 (February 1910): 5–12, 41–47.

11. The Art Institute of Chicago, the Metropolitan Museum, and the New-York Historical Society were the only institutions that participated in the Dutch paintings exhibition. W. R. Valentiner, *Catalogue of a Collection of Paintings by Dutch Masters of the Seventeenth Century*, volume one of *The Hudson-Fulton Celebration, Catalogue of an Exhibition Held in the Metropolitan Museum of Art* (New York: Metropolitan Museum of Art, 1909), v–vi. In 1924, a decade after his father's death, J. P. (Jack) Morgan, Jr., created the public institution known today as the Morgan Library & Museum.

12. "London to See Old Masters," *The New York Times*, October 3. 1909, C3. Courtesy of the New York State Library. Kenyon Cox in *The Burlington Magazine* quoted in Quodbach, 29.

13. "Famous Art Works Coming to New York," *The New York Times*, September 15, 1909, 5. "Art at Home and Abroad," *The New York Times*, October 3, 1909, X3. "Altman Back From Europe," *The New York Times*, September 22, 1909, 3. At his death in 1913, Altman left his Dutch paintings to the Metropolitan Museum. "Benjamin Altman Dies, Leaves $45,000,000," *The New York Times*, October 8, 1913, 1. Courtesy of the New York State Library.

14. Burt, 315.

15. "Art at Home and Abroad," *The New York Times*, October 10, 1909, SM 12. "Art at Home and Abroad," *The New York Times*, September 9, 1909, X3. Courtesy of the New York State Library. Curtis, "The Hudson-Fulton Memorial Art Exhibit in New York," 140. "Address by de Forest," quoted in Wendy Kaplan, "R. T. H. Halsey: An Ideology of Collecting American Decorative Arts," *Winterthur Portfolio* 17 (Spring 1982): 46. Burt, 315. See also: Frances Gruber Safford, "The Hudson-Fulton Exhibition and H. Eugene Bolles, New York Metropolitan Museum, American Wing," *The Magazine Antiques* 157 (January 2000): 170–175 and Amelia Peck, "Robert de Forest and the Founding of the American Wing," *The Magazine Antiques* 157 (January 2000): 175–181.

16. "Christian Activities in New York," *New-York Observer*, September 30, 1909, 443. Courtesy of the New York State Library. Hall, *The Hudson-Fulton Celebration 1909*, 1:183-184, 183. *John Sloan's New York Scene: From the Diaries, Notes and Correspondence 1906–1913.* ed. Bruce St. John (New York, Harper &

Row, 1965), 340–341, 344, 348. Bernice Kert, *Abby Aldrich Rockefeller: The Woman in the Family* (New York: Random House, 1993), 131.

17. Hall, *The Hudson-Fulton Celebration 1909*, 1:175.

18. Hall, *The Hudson-Fulton Celebration 1909*, 1:195.

19. Called "Dirty Kate" during her life, and possibly insane due to syphilis, Corbin and her image were spiffed up and presented as an example of true womanhood during an era of colonial revival and of contested rights and roles for women. Howard Zinn, *A People's History of the United States* (1980; reprint, New York: Perennial Classics, 2003), 110. Hall, *The Hudson-Fulton Celebration 1909*, 1:383–384, 427.

20. Hall, *The Hudson-Fulton Celebration 1909*, 1:16–17, 413–414. "A Great Bridge in Honor of Henry Hudson," *The New York Times*, July 11, 1906, SM6. Courtesy of the New York State Library. Lincoln Diamant, *Hoopla on the Hudson, An Intimate View of New York's Great 1909 Hudson-Fulton Celebration* (Fleischmanns, NY: Purple Mountain Press, 2003), 13, 21n., 14.

21. Hall, *The Hudson-Fulton Celebration 1909*, 1:394–399.

22. Hall, *The Hudson-Fulton Celebration 1909*, 1:392–412. George F. Kunz, "Address Given at Conference on the Conservation of Natural Resources" (1912), 408–418, in The Evolution of the Conservation Movement, 1850–1920. http://memory.loc.gov/cgi-bin (accessed on January 3, 2008).

Symbols, Souvenirs & Sales

1. Advertisement for Browning, King & Co., *The New York Times*, September 28, 1909, 4. Advertisement for Pianola Pianos, *The New York Times*, September 27, 1909, 3. Advertisement for A. A. Vantine & Co., *The New York Times*, September 28, 1909, 4. Courtesy of the New York State Library.

2. Edward Hagaman Hall, *The Hudson-Fulton Celebration 1909, The Fourth Annual Report of the Hudson-Fulton Celebration Commission to the Legislature of the State of New York, Transmitted to the Legislature May Twentieth, Nineteen Ten*, 2 vols. (Albany: J. B. Lyon Company, 1910), 1:75–88. The Commission also created a seal and invited the U.S. Post Office to issue a stamp.

3. Hall, *The Hudson-Fulton Celebration 1909*, 1:77–84. Advertisement for Abraham & Straus, *The New York Times*, September 5, 1909, x12. Advertisement for Macy's, *The New York Times*, September 5, 1909, C1. Advertisement for Abraham & Straus, *The New York Times*, September 5, 1909, X12. Courtesy of the New York State Museum.

4. Hall, *The Hudson-Fulton Celebration 1909*, 1:97.

5. Hall, *The Hudson-Fulton Celebration 1909*, 1:86.

6. "No Cause for Indignation," *The New York Times*, October 1, 1909, 8. Courtesy of the New York State Library.

7. Hall, *The Hudson-Fulton Celebration 1909*, 1:84–85.

8. Hall, *The Hudson-Fulton Celebration 1909*, 1:5. Advertisement for Redfield Brothers, *The New York Times*, September 17, 1909, 2. Courtesy of the New York State Library. Hall, *The Hudson-Fulton Celebra-*

tion 1909, 1:88–89. At least one other firm with an official license found itself in a similar situation. Months after the Celebration's conclusion, Whitehead & Hoag complained that the Commission owed it $24,000. "Hudson-Fulton Bill Unpaid," *The New York Times*, January 21, 1910, 7. Courtesy of the New York State Library.

9. Elbert Hubbard, the founder of the Roycroft Press and the author of the essay on Henry Hudson contained in the book, quoted from Root's speech as transcribed in "Fulton Dinner of 36 Nations," *The New York Times*, September 1, 1909, 1. Courtesy of the New York State Library. Perhaps prompted by the excitement leading up to the Celebration, Elbert Hubbard published a Roycroft Press edition of Washington Irving's *Rip Van Winkle* in 1906.

10. Rudolph Diamant, news dispatches dated September 22, 1909 and September 2, 1909 in Lincoln Diamant, *Hoopla on the Hudson: An Intimate View of New York's Great 1909 Hudson-Fulton Celebration* (Fleischmanns, NY: Purple Mountain Press, 2003), 61, 44. "How the Souvenir Habit is Affecting Banquets, Interesting Facts Showing the Extent of Fad in Hudson-Fulton Celebration," *The New York Times*, October 10, 1909, SM7. Courtesy of the New York State Library.

11. Advertisement for Macy's, *The New York Times*, September 23, 1909, 5. Advertisement for Christman Sons, *The New York Times*, September 25, 1909, 19. Advertisement for Simpson Crawford Company, *The New York Times*, September 25, 1909, 3. "Hudson-Fulton Sale of Best Groceries," Advertisement for Bloomingdale's Department Store, *The New York Times*, September 26, 1909, xi. Advertisement for Bloomingdale's Department Store, *The New York Times*, September 1, 1909, 5. Advertisement for Abraham & Straus, *The New York Times*, September 29, 1909, X10. Advertisement for O'Neill-Adam Company, *The New York Times*, October 29, 1909, 5. "Odd Fulton Illuminations," *The New York Times*, October 3, 1909, 4. Courtesy of the New York State Library.

Air & Sea, Peace & War

1. *A Maritime History of New York, Compiled by the Workers of the Writers Program of the Work Projects Administration For the City of New York*, introduction by Fiorello H. La Guardia (Garden City, NY: Doubleday, Duran & Co., 1941), 219–220.

2. Brooks McNamara, *Day of Jubilee: The Great Age of Public Celebrations in New York, 1788–1909* (New Brunswick, NJ: Rutgers University Press, 1997), 22–24, 48, 140–143, 143–146, 147–148, 149–154, 155–157. "Parade for Dewey Outdone By Far," *New York Herald*, September 25, 1909, 4. Courtesy of the New York State Library.

3. Edward Hagaman Hall, *The Hudson-Fulton Celebration 1909, The Fourth Annual Report of the Hudson-Fulton Celebration Commission to the Legislature of the State of New York, Transmitted to the Legislature May Twentieth, Nineteen Ten*, 2 vols. (Albany: J. B. Lyon Company, 1910) 1:93–103. "Hudson's Cabin, Four Feet High, Opened for Many Sightseers," *New York Herald*, September 24, 1909, 6. "Up-Hudson Cities Take Celebration," *The New York Times*, October 4, 1909, 3. Courtesy of the New York State Library.

4. Hall, *The Hudson-Fulton Celebration 1909*, 1:105–114. The boat was first, and erroneously, called the *Clermont* by Cadwallader Colden in his 1817 biography of Fulton. Kirkpatrick Sale, *The Fire of His Genius: Robert Fulton and the American Dream* (New York: The Free Press, 2001), 21. Hall, *The Hudson-Fulton Celebration 1909*, 1:113. "Clermont Once More Floats in the Bay," *The New York Times*, July 11, 1909, 12. Courtesy of the New York State Library.

5. *Historical Pageant, Hudson-Fulton Celebration, September 25 to October 9, 1909* (New York: printed for the Hudson-Fulton Celebration Commission by Redfield Brothers, 1909), 53. "A Record Torpedo Shot," *The New York Times*, August 26, 1909, 1. Courtesy of the New York State Library. Hall, 1:205.

6. "Millions of Persons Join in Opening Ceremonies of the Great Celebration," *New York Herald*, September 26, 1909, 1. Courtesy of the New York State Library. Hall, *The Hudson-Fulton Celebration 1909*, 1:204–229. Gustav Kobbé, *Hudson-Fulton Celebration: 1909* (New York: Society of Iconophiles, 1910), 31–32. "Famous Water Parade Starts Big Celebration," *New York Press*, September 26, 1909, 1–2, 2. Courtesy of the New York State Library.

7. "Millions of Persons Join in Opening Ceremonies of the Great Celebration," *New York Herald*, September 26, 1909, 1. Courtesy of the New York State Library. Hall, *The Hudson-Fulton Celebration 1909*, 1:204, 232–233. "Sightseers Use Roofs; Boat Owners Suffer," *New York Press*, September 26, 1909, 1. Courtesy of the New York State Library. *John Sloan's New York Scene: From the Diaries, Notes and Correspondence 1906–1913*, ed. Bruce St. John (New York, Harper & Row, 1965), 336. Hall, *The Hudson-Fulton Celebration 1909*, 1:205.

8. Kobbé, 27, 37. "Echoes of the Naval Parade," *The Evening Post*, September 27, 1909, 4. Courtesy of the New York State Library.

9. Hall, *The Hudson-Fulton Celebration 1909*, 1:123.

10. *John Sloan's New York Scene*, 335.

11. Henry Reuterdahl, "The Needs of Our Navy," *McClure's Magazine* (January 1908): 251–263. "Our Need of Better Warships," *The New York Times*, December 25, 1907, 6. Courtesy of the New York State Library.

12. Hall, *The Hudson-Fulton Celebration, 1909*, 1: 198–199, 2: 1139. An editorial pointed out that the Hudson-Fulton inaugural Naval Parade demonstrated that American warships were not equal to British vessels and urged those in charge of the American fleet to encourage innovation. Editorial page, *The Evening Post*, September 27, 1909, 6. "Fulton Dinner of 36 Nations," *The New York Times*, September 30, 1909, 1. "Aviators Will Fly Over City Today," *New York Call*, September 27, 1909, 1–2. Courtesy of the New York State Library.

13. "Famous Water Parade Starts Big Celebration," *New York Press*, September 26, 1909, 1–2, 1. "Hudson-Fulton Day," *The Evening Post*, September 25, 1909, 1. "102 Socialists in Crew of Utrecht," *New York Call*, September 25, 1909, 3. "Aviators Will Fly Over City Today," *New York Call*, September 27, 1909, 1–2. Courtesy of the New York State Library.

14. "War and Peace," *New York Call*, September 27, 1909, 6. "Peace Flag Salute Will Open Parade," *New York Herald*, September 25, 1909, 6. "Long-Range Fulton Show," *The New York Times*, October 7, 1909, 4. Editorial, *The Evening Post*, September 22, 1909, 8.

Courtesy of the New York State Library. Receptions for officers were held at Governor's Island, West Point, and Columbia University. Hall, *The Hudson-Fulton Celebration 1909*, 1:278–281, 2:852–858. "Jackies in Races on River," *The Evening Post*, September 29, 1909, 1. "The Academy of Music in Brooklyn was the scene of an international reception and subscription ball in the evening [of the Military Parade] at which twenty-seven nations were formally represented. The admirals of all the visiting squadrons were there, as well as officers of the American fleet and army." "Martial Parade Surpasses Week's Historic Events," *New York Press*, October 1, 1909, 1, 3. Courtesy of the New York State Library. Hall, *The Hudson-Fulton Celebration 1909*, 2:851. "Railroad Courtesies for Visiting Tars," *The New York Times*, September 14, 1909, 3. Courtesy of the New York State Library.

15. "Millions Cheer Martial Pomp," *The New York Times*, October 1, 1909, 1. "The Military Parade," *The Evening Post*, October 1, 1909, 6. "Hudson-Fulton Fête to Be Militaristic," *New York Call*, September 22, 1909, 2. "Military Pageant," *Daily People*, October 1, 1909, 1. Courtesy of the New York State Library.

16. "Sky Sailors Take Their Own Time," *New York Herald*, September 24, 1909, 6. Courtesy of the New York State Library. Hall, *The Hudson-Fulton Celebration 1909*, 1:486–490. "Wright to Attempt Long Flights Here, Signs a Contract with H-F Committee," *The New York Times*, August 24, 1909, 2. "Luncheon for Curtiss," *The New York Times*, September 2, 1909, 4. "Curtiss's Career in Aeronautics," *The New York Times*, May 30, 1910, 6. "Wright to Start Suit on Curtiss Airship," *The New York Times*, August 20, 1909, 2. Courtesy of the New York State Library.

17. "A Seeing New York Airship Expects to Carry Passengers over Town from an Aeronautic Show," *The New York Times*, September 22, 1909, 1. "Air Ship to Fly into New York," *New York Herald*, September 21, 1909, p. 6. "Hudson-Fulton Flights to Be the Most Perilous Ever Undertaken," *New York Herald*, September 19, 1909, section 3, page 5. "Prize Winning Aeroplane on View," *New-York Tribune*, September 28, 1909, 4. Courtesy of the New York State Library. Hall, *The Hudson-Fulton Celebration 1909*, 1:489–490.

18. "Albany Balloon Effort Later," *The Evening Post*, September 27, 1909, 1. "Wilbur Wright Circles The Statue of Liberty in Aeroplane," *New York Herald*, September 30, 1909, 4. "Aeroplanes Fly, Dirigibles Fail, In City's Celebration," *New York Press*, September 30, 1909, 1–2, 2. "Wilbur Wright Sails over the Hudson for Twenty Miles In the Most Spectacular Aeroplane Flight on Record," *New York Herald*, October 5, 1909, 5. "Day of Air Flights," *The Evening Post*, September 29, 1909, 1, 14. "Aeroplanes Did Not Rise," *The Evening Post*, September 28, 1909, 1. Courtesy of the New York State Library.

19. "Day of Air Flights," *The Evening Post*, September 29, 1909, 1, 14. "Balloonists Fail," *New York Call*, September 30, 1909, 2.

Up the River

1. "Aldermen in Tight Embrace," *New-York Tribune*, September 23, 1909, 5. "Brooklyn Parade Proved A Fizzle," *The New York Times*, October 2, 1909, 2. "Parade in Confusion," *New-York Tribune*, October 2, 1909, 5. Courtesy of the New York State Library.

Edward Hagaman Hall, *The Hudson-Fulton Celebration 1909, The Fourth Annual Report of the Hudson-Fulton Celebration Commission to the Legislature of the State of New York, Transmitted to the Legislature May Twentieth, Nineteen Ten*, 2 vols. (Albany: J. B. Lyon Company, 1910), 2:894. "Floats Miss Parade in Poughkeepsie," *The New York Times*, October 5, 1909, 5. "Battered Floats in Albany's Parade," *The New York Times*, October 9, 1909, 4. "Float Blazes Up in Brooklyn Parade," *The New York Times*, October 10, 1909, 1. Courtesy of the New York State Library. Hall, *The Hudson-Fulton Celebration 1909*, 2:720–721, 722–723.

2. "Staten Island Has a Fulton Dinner," *The New York Times*, October 1, 1909, 2. Courtesy of the New York State Library. Hall, *The Hudson-Fulton Celebration 1909*, 2:764–777, 763, 778–780, 793, 797, 814–816.

3. *Official Program, Hudson-Fulton Celebration* (New York: Printed for the Hudson-Fulton Celebration Commission by Redfield Brothers, 1909), 11–12. Hall, *The Hudson-Fulton Celebration 1909*, 2:1029, 903–905.

4. Hall, *The Hudson-Fulton Celebration 1909*, 2:907–908.

5. For example, the Ossining commemorative booklet featured paid advertisements, biographies of prominent businesspeople, and histories of local businesses. *Hudson-Fulton Celebration, October 7, 1909, Ossining-on-Hudson* (Ossining, NY: Physioc Press, 1909).

6. For example, see Hall, *The Hudson-Fulton Celebration 1909*, 2:1004–1013. This official report contains the texts of many speeches delivered during the Celebration.

7. http://cowhampshire.blogharbor.com (accessed March 8, 2008). Hall, *The Hudson-Fulton Celebration 1909*, 2:941. Edward Watkinson Rankin to Herbert E. Rankin, Albany, September 29, 1909, Series 8. Historic Cherry Hill, Albany, NY.

8. Hall, *The Hudson-Fulton Celebration 1909*, 2:930–931, 1015. Margaret L. Vetare, *Philipsburg Manor, Upper Mills* (Tarrytown, NY: Historic Hudson Valley Press, 2004), 60 n. http://www.nps.gov/history/history/online_books/explorers/sitec48.htm (accessed December 7, 2007). Philipse Manor Hall opened as a museum in 1912.

9. Hall, *The Hudson-Fulton Celebration 1909*, 1:354–355, 356. The convicts had chopped many cords of firewood to power the *Clermont*. "Convicts See Naval Parade," *The Evening Post*, October 1, 1909, 1. "Upper Hudson Joins in the Celebration," *The New York Times*, October 2, 1909, 1. Courtesy of the New York State Library. Hall, *The Hudson-Fulton Celebration 1909*, 1:360, 926. Newburgh's festivities also included a land parade.

10. Hall, *The Hudson-Fulton Celebration 1909*, 2:907, 890–892, 909.

11. Hall, *The Hudson-Fulton Celebration 1909*, 2:896-898. "Crew of Half Moon in Catskill Haunt," *The New York Times*, October 7, 1909, 5. Courtesy of the New York State Library. Hall, *The Hudson-Fulton Celebration 1909*, 2:894, 905–906. Croton's parade was not part of the Commission's official roster of events.

12. Edward Rankin referred to October 8 as Albany's "great day." Edward Watkinson Rankin to Herbert E. Rankin, Albany, September 29, 1909, Series 8. Historic Cherry Hill, Albany, NY. Hall, *The Hudson-Fulton Celebration 1909*, 2:926, 929.

13. "Great Crowd at Poughkeepsie," *The New York Times*, October 4, 1909, 3. "Kingston Honors Chambers," *The New York Times*, October 5, 1909, 5. "Gov. Hughes Makes Record," *The New York Times*, October 6, 1909, 1. "The Hudson-Fulton Celebration," *New-York Observer*, September 23, 1909, 409. "Up-Hudson Cities Take Celebration," *The New York Times*, October 4, 1909, 3. Courtesy of the New York State Library. Hall, *The Hudson-Fulton Celebration 1909*, 2:1002.

14. Hall, *The Hudson-Fulton Celebration 1909*, 2:1015, 1019–1020. *Albany Institute of History & Art, 200 Years of Collecting*, ed. Tammis K. Groft and Mary Alice Mackay (New York: Hudson Hills Press and Albany Institute of History & Art, 1998), 29. Hall, *The Hudson-Fulton Celebration 1909*, 2:1051–1052, 1060; 1:124.

15. Hall, *The Hudson-Fulton Celebration 1909*, 2:1085–1090, 1091–1092.

The Party's Over

1. "Statue of Purity for Times Square," *The New York Times*, October 5, 1909, 1. "Miss Gotham Feels as if She is Miscast," *The New York Times*, October 10, 1909, 10. "Miss Purity Displaced," *The New York Times*, November 22, 1909, 2. [New York's Fair Name], *The Evening Post*, October 5, 1909, 6. Courtesy of the New York State Library.

2. "Overbalancing Event with Record," *The New York Times*, May 16, 1911, 12. Courtesy of the New York State Library. Edward Hagaman Hall, *The Hudson-Fulton Celebration 1909, The Fourth Annual Report of the Hudson-Fulton Celebration Commission to the Legislature of the State of New York, Transmitted to the Legislature May Twentieth, Nineteen Ten*, 2 vols. (Albany: J. B. Lyon Company, 1910), 1:45–57, 46–47, 48. "Pageant Figures Sold," *The New York Times*, July 28, 1910, 6. Courtesy of the New York State Library. Gustav Stickley, "Als Ik Kan, Selling a City for Five Hundred Million Dollars," *The Craftsman* 22 (July 1912): 459–461, 459. http://digicoll.library.wisc.edu (accessed August 30, 2007).

3. Hall, *The Hudson-Fulton Celebration, 1909*, 2:1112–1135. "Clermont's Fate Undecided," *The New York Times*, July 11, 1910, 5. Courtesy of the New York State Library.

4. "Disposition of Ships," *The New York Times*, September 29, 1909, 10. "Brooklyn Loses Half Moon," *The New York Times*, June 11, 1910, 5. Courtesy of the New York State Library. Lincoln Diamant, *Hoopla on the Hudson: An Intimate View of New York's Great 1909 Hudson-Fulton Celebration* (Fleischmanns, NY: Purple Mountain Press, 2003), 122–125. Thomas Rinaldi, "The Hudson's Lost Steam Fleet," *Steamboat Bill* (Fall 2003): 173–193, 187–189. I am grateful to Ray Armater for sharing information about the Hudson River Day Line's purchase and display of the *Clermont*.

5. The tomb was not an official Hudson-Fulton Celebration project but was under development before, during, and after the Celebration. "New York's $3,000,000 Robert Fulton Memorial," *The New York Times*, October 22, 1910, SM5. Courtesy of the New York State Library.

6. "Rip, Robert and Hendrick and 1909," *Daily People*, September 26, 1909, 4. "Mr. Bigelow's Protest," *New York Tribune*, September 17, 1909, 5. Courtesy of the New York State Library.

7. Editorial "Hudson and Fulton," *New York Call*, September 25, 1909, 1. Courtesy of the New York State Library.

8. *The Encyclopedia of New York City*, ed. Kenneth T. Jackson (New Haven, CT: Yale University Press; New York: New-York Historical Society, 1995), 583, 1199.

9. Emma Lazarus authored her most famous poem for an auction to raise money for the Statue of Liberty in 1883. It was one of many literary works sold at the time. The Quota Act of 1921 was the first federal immigration law to reduce mass migration to the United States. It limited the number of foreign nationals entering the United States to 3% of each nationality represented in the 1910 census. The Immigration Act of 1924 restricted admissions to 2% of each nationality living in the United States in 1890 and the National Origins Act of 1929 made the quotas permanent. I am grateful to Judy Giuriceo-Lord, curator of exhibits and media at the Statue of Liberty and Ellis Island Immigration Museum of the National Park Service, for sharing information and insights with me.

10. For example, see "Celebration's Guiding Spirit," *The New York Times*, October 3, 1909, 12. Untitled [From the Artistic Point of View], *The Evening Post*, October 5, 1909, 6. Courtesy of the New York State Library.

11. "Curtiss's Career in Aeronautics," *The New York Times*, May 30, 1910, 6. Courtesy of the New York State Library.

12. *The Encyclopedia of New York City*, 1074. "'City of Dreadful Height,'" *The New York Times*, September 26, 1909, 5. Courtesy of the New York State Library.

13. "Farewell Dinner to the Admirals," *The New York Times*, October 8, 1909, 6. Courtesy of the New York State Library.

14. Hall, *The Hudson-Fulton Celebration 1909*, 2:1074–1075.

15. Stephen Chalmers, "Looking Ahead to a Celebration in the Year 2009," *The New York Times*, September 26, 1909, MD12. Courtesy of the New York State Library.

16. Later in his career, Chalmers wrote about tuberculosis and its effect on the lives of writer Robert Louis Stevenson, medical researcher and sanitarium director Dr. Edward Livingston Trudeau, and others.

Bibliography

Books and Periodicals

1609–1909, The Dutch in New Netherland and the United States. New York: The Netherland Chamber of Commerce, 1909.

Appleton's Cyclopedia of American Biography. Edited by James Grant Wilson and John Riske. 6 volumes. New York: D. Appleton and Company, 1887.

Binnewies, Robert O. *Palisades: 100,000 Acres in 100 Years.* New York: Fordham University Press and Palisades Interstate Park Commission, 2001.

Burrows, Edwin G. and Mike Wallace. *Gotham: A History of New York City to 1898.* New York and Oxford: Oxford University Press, 1999.

Burt, Nathaniel. *Palaces for the People: A Social History of the American Art Museum.* Boston: Little, Brown & Company, 1977.

Clarke, J. I. C. and E. Hubbard. *Manhattan and Henry Hudson.* East Aurora, NY: Roycroft Press, 1910.

Curtis, Natalie. "The Hudson-Fulton Memorial Art Exhibit in New York." *The Craftsman* 17 (November 1909): 124–141.

Dearstyne, Bruce W. "Archival Politics in New York State, 1892–1915." *New York History* 66, no. 2 (April 1985): 164–184.

Descriptive Guide to the Grounds, Buildings and Collections and Native Trees of the Hudson River Valley. New York: Hudson-Fulton Celebration Commission and The New York Botanical Garden Bronx Park, 1909.

Diamant, Lincoln. *Hoopla on the Hudson: An Intimate View of New York's Great Celebration of 1909.* Fleischmanns, NY: Purple Mountain Press, 2003.

Dickinson, H. W. *Robert Fulton: Engineer and Artist, His Life and Works.* London: John Lane, 1913.

Dunlap, William. *A History of New York, For Schools.* 2 volumes. New York: Collins, Keese, & Co., 1837.

The Encyclopedia of New York City. Edited by Kenneth T. Jackson. New Haven, CT: Yale University Press; New York: New-York Historical Society, 1995.

Gordon, Linda. *The Moral Property of Women: A History of Birth Control Politics in America.* Urbana and Chicago: University of Illinois Press, 2002.

Hall, Edward Hagaman. *Hudson and Fulton, A Brief History of Henry Hudson and Robert Fulton with Suggestions Designed To Aid the Holding of General Commemorative Exercises and Children's Festivals During the Hudson-Fulton Celebration in 1909.* New York: The Hudson-Fulton Celebration Commission, 1909.

———. *The Hudson-Fulton Celebration 1909, The Fourth Annual Report of the Hudson-Fulton Celebration to the Legislature of the State of New York, Transmitted to the Legislature May Twentieth, Nineteen Ten.* 2 volumes. Albany, NY: J. B. Lyon Company, 1910.

Hamilton, Milton W. *Henry Hudson and the Dutch in New York.* Albany, NY: University of the State of New York, 1959.

Historical Pageant, Hudson-Fulton Celebration, September 25 to October 9, 1909. New York: Printed for the Hudson-Fulton Celebration Commission by Redfield Brothers, 1909.

Historical Souvenir of the Hudson-Fulton Celebration. New York: New York Commercial, 1909.

Horner, Harlan Hoyt. Hudson-Fulton Celebration, September 25 to October 9, 1909. Albany, NY: New York State Education Department, 1909.

The Hudson-Fulton Celebration Booklet. New York: Public Health and Convenience Committee of the Hudson-Fulton Celebration Commission, 1909.

"Hudson-Fulton Celebration Issue." Scientific American 101, no. 13 (September 25, 1909). Special Edition.

Hudson-Fulton Celebration, October 7, 1909, Ossining-on-Hudson. Ossining, NY: Physioc Press, 1909.

"Hudson-Fulton Celebration: Warship Supplement." The Master, Mate & Pilot 2, no. 5 (October 1909). Special Edition.

"Hudson-Fulton Number." Judge 57, no. 1457 (September 18, 1909). Special Edition.

Irving, Washington. A History of New York. Edited by Michael L. Black and Nancy B. Black. Boston: Twayne Publishers, 1984.

Jastrow, Marie. Looking Back: The American Dream Through Immigrant Eyes. New York and London: W. W. Norton & Co., Inc., 1986.

John Sloan's New York Scene: From the Diaries, Notes and Correspondence, 1906–1913. Edited by Bruce St. John. New York: Harper & Row, 1965.

Johnson, Donald S. Charting the Sea of Darkness: The Four Voyages of Henry Hudson. Camden, ME: International Marine, 1993.

Johnson, Kathleen Eagen. "From Frans Hals to Windmills: The Arts and Crafts Fascination with the Culture of the Low Countries." In Substance of Style: Perspectives on the American Arts and Crafts Movement, edited by Bert Denker. Winterthur, DE: Henry Francis du Pont Winterthur Museum, 1996, 47–67.

Kaplan, Wendy. "R. T. H. Halsey: An Ideology of Collecting American Decorative Arts." Winterthur Portfolio 17, no.1 (Spring 1982): 43–54.

Kent, Henry Watson and Florence N. Levy. The Hudson-Fulton Celebration MCMIX: The Metropolitan Museum of Art Exhibition. Vol. 2, Catalogue of an Exhibition of American Paintings, Furniture, Silver, and Other Objects of Art. New York: The Metropolitan Museum of Art, 1909.

Kert, Bernice. Abby Aldrich Rockefeller: The Woman in the Family. New York: Random House, 1993.

Kimmelman, Barbara. "Design and Construction of the IRT: Electrical Engineering." Survey Number Historical American Engineering Record, NY-22, National Park Service, 283–363, http://www.nycsubway.org/articles/haer-design-electrical.html.

Kobbé, Gustav. Hudson-Fulton Celebration: 1909. New York: Society of Bibliophiles, 1910.

Lewis, Tom. The Hudson: A History. New Haven and London: Yale University Press, 2005.

List of Prints, Books, Manuscripts, Etc. Relating to Henry Hudson, the Hudson River, Robert Fulton and Steam Navigation. New York: New York Public Library and the Hudson-Fulton Celebration Commission, 1909.

Mack, Arthur C. The Palisades of the Hudson. Edgewater, NJ: The Palisade Press, 1909.

Mahan, Harold E. Benson J. Lossing and Historical Writing in the United States, 1830–1890. Westport, CT: Greenwood Press, 1996.

A Maritime History of New York, Compiled by the Workers of the Writers Program of the Work Projects Administration for the City of New York. Introduction by Fiorello H. La Guardia. Garden City, NY: Doubleday, Duran & Co., 1941.

Marling, Karal Ann. George Washington Slept Here. Cambridge, MA and London: Harvard University Press, 1988.

McNamara, Brooks. Day of Jubilee: The Great Age of Public Celebrations in New York, 1788–1909. New Brunswick, NJ: Rutgers University Press, 1997.

Meany, Joseph H., Jr. "New York: The State of History." Essay compiled in 1994 and revised in 2001, http://www.nysm.nysed.gov/services/meanydoc.html.

Melville, Norbert John. Hudson-Fulton Pageant of Dramatization: A Typical Pageant of United States History. New York: Hinds, Noble & Eldredge, 1909.

Molson, Francis J. "The Boy Inventor in American Series Fiction, 1900–1930." Journal of Popular Fiction 28 (1994): 31–48.

Official Program, Hudson-Fulton Celebration. New York: Printed for the Hudson-Fulton Celebration Commission by Redfield Brothers, 1909.

Official Robert Fulton Exhibition of the Hudson-Fulton Commission. New York: The New-York Historical Society and the Colonial Dames of America, 1909.

Peck, Amelia. "Robert de Forest and the Founding of the American Wing." The Magazine Antiques 157, no.1 (January 2000): 176–181.

Philip, Cynthia Owen. Robert Fulton: A Biography. New York: Franklin Watts, 1985.

Quodbach, Esmée. "The Age of Rembrandt: Dutch Paintings in the Metropolitan Museum of Art." Metropolitan Museum of Art Bulletin (Summer 2007). Reprint, New Haven and London: Yale University Press, 2007.

Reuterdahl, Henry. "The Needs of Our Navy." McClure's Magazine (January 1908): 251–263.

Rhodes, William. "Colonial Revival and the Americanization of Immigrants." In The Colonial Revival in America, edited by Alan Axelrod. New York: W. W. Norton & Company, 1985, 341–361.

Safford, Frances Gruber. "The Hudson-Fulton Exhibition and H. Eugene Bolles, New York Metropolitan Museum, American Wing." *The Magazine Antiques* 157, no. 1 (January 2000): 170–175.

Sale, Kirkpatrick. *The Fire of His Genius: Robert Fulton and the American Dream.* New York: The Free Press, 1981.

Sandler, Corey. *Henry Hudson: Dreams and Obsessions.* New York: Citadel Press Books, 2007.

Skinner, Alanson. "The Indians of Manhattan Island and Vicinity." *American Museum Journal* 9, no. 6 (September 1909): 143–193.

Stickley, Gustav. "The People and the Pageant." *The Craftsman* 17 (November 1909): 223–7.

Strouse, Jean. *Morgan: American Financier.* New York: Random House, 1999.

Sweeting, Adam W. *Reading Houses and Building Books: Andrew Jackson Downing and the Architecture of Popular Antebellum Literature, 1835–1855.* Hanover, NH: University Press of New England, 1996.

Tercentenary of the Hudson and Centennial of the Steamboat. Walden, NY: The Wallkill Valley Publishing Association, 1909.

Vail, R. W. G. *Knickerbocker Birthday: A Sesqui-Centennial History of the New York Historical Society, 1804–1954.* New York: The New-York Historical Society, 1954.

Valentiner, W. R. *The Hudson-Fulton Celebration MCMIX: The Metropolitan Museum of Art Exhibition.* Vol. 1, *Catalogue of a Collection of Paintings by Dutch Masters of the Seventeenth Century.* New York: The Metropolitan Museum of Art, 1909.

Von Drehle, David. *Triangle: The Fire That Changed America.* New York: Atlantic Monthly Press, 2003.

Wessler, Robert. *Charles Evans Hughes: Politics and Reform in New York, 1905–1910.* Ithaca, NY: Cornell University Press, 1967.

Williams, Stanley T. and Mary Allen Edge. *A Bibliography of the Writings of Washington Irving, A Check List.* 1936. Reprint, New York: Burt Franklin, 1970.

Zangwill, Israel. *The Melting Pot, A Drama in Four Acts.* New York: Macmillan, 1919.

Zinn, Howard. 1980. *A People's History of the United States, 1492–Present.* 1980. Reprint, New York: Perennial Classics, 2003.

Newspapers

August 1909 through October 1909.

Daily People.

The Evening Post.

The Irish-American.

New York Call.

New York Herald.

New-York Observer.

New York Press.

The New York Times.

New-York Tribune.

New York World.

Rural New Yorker.

The Sun.

Wall Street Summary.

Weekly People.

Manuscript Collections

Daughters of the American Revolution, Hendrick Hudson Chapter papers. Hudson, NY.

Hudson-Fulton Celebration collection. Croton-on-Hudson Historical Society, Croton, NY.

Hudson-Fulton Celebration collection. Field Library, Peekskill, NY.

Hudson-Fulton Celebration collection. Peekskill Museum, Peekskill, NY.

Rankin Family papers. Historic Cherry Hill, Albany, NY.

Rockefeller, John D., Jr., papers. Rockefeller Archive Center, Sleepy Hollow, NY.

Sutcliffe, Alice Crary. "Robert Fulton, the Man, A Talk, Illustrated with Lantern Guides." Lecture, typescript, 1909–1910. Clermont State Historic Site, Germantown, NY.

Appendix 1: Hudson-Fulton Celebration Calendar of Activities

This is a transcription of the day-by-day listing that appeared in souvenir publications issued by the Commission.

PROGRAM OF EVENTS

The Hudson-Fulton Celebration will take place from Saturday, Sept. 25, to Saturday, Oct. 9, 1909. The principal events during the first eight days will occur in Greater New York and upon the Hudson River opposite the city. In the following week the Celebration will continue at the Hudson River cities and villages from Yonkers to Troy.

GENERAL PUBLIC CEREMONIES

The schedule of the principal events upon city streets and the Hudson River includes the following:

SATURDAY, SEPT. 25: Rendezvous of American and foreign naval vessels at New York; Naval Parade encircling the fleet of war vessels and reception of Official Guests at 110th Street and Riverside Park in afternoon; in evening, illuminated Naval Parade, encircling the war fleet. On this evening and succeeding evenings during the celebration there will be a remarkable series of illuminations of public buildings, line of parade, Riverside and fleet. On this day will occur the religious observances of those accustomed to worship on Saturday.

SUNDAY, SEPT. 26: Religious observances by those accustomed to worship on Sunday.

MONDAY, SEPT. 27: Official receptions to guests, opening of exhibitions in places subsequently to be announced and beginning of airship flights.

TUESDAY, SEPT. 28: Historical Parade and Pageant, participated in by all nationalities; procession of floats and moving tableaux representing principal events in history of Aboriginal, Dutch, English, Revolutionary and American Periods.

WEDNESDAY, SEPT. 29: Aquatic Sports, opposite Riverside Park and Yonkers; General Commemorative Exercises in educational institutions throughout the State; also dedication of memorials throughout the State; ceremonies of 'Bronx Borough Day' in that Borough; Children's Festivals in Richmond Borough; reception by U.S. authorities to Official Guests at West Point.

THURSDAY, SEPT. 30: Military Parade in Manhattan Borough, participated in by U.S. Army, Navy and Marine Corps, National Guard, Naval Militia, veteran organizations and marines and sailors from foreign vessels.

FRIDAY, OCT. 1: Naval Parade of naval vessels, merchant marine, excursion boats, pleasure craft, etc., in two divisions, one starting from New York and the other from Albany, meeting at Newburg [sic]; reception of the fleet in Newburg Bay; ceremonies upon Half Moon and Clermont joining Upper Hudson Division; Newburg street parade, reception of Official Guests, with illuminations and fireworks in evening. The Manhattan Historical Parade will be repeated in Brooklyn.

SATURDAY, OCT. 2: Children's Festivals in 50 centres in Greater New York, conducted in view of 500,000 school children; return of two divisions of Naval Parade from Newburg; Manhattan Historical Parade repeated on Staten Island; Dedicatory Exercises at Stony Point. In the evening there will be a great Carnival Parade in Manhattan, with 50 brilliantly illuminated floats, escorted by various organizations.

SATURDAY, OCT. 9: Similar Carnival Parade in Brooklyn Borough, on Eastern Parkway, from 8 to 11 p.m.

UPPER HUDSON CELEBRATION

The Celebration will be continued on the Hudson River north of New York City throughout the second week, from Oct. 3 to Oct. 9. Special ceremonies, with the historical floats in parades, will occur in all the river cities and larger villages, with neighboring smaller municipalities participating in each of them.

Monday, Oct. 4, will be the chief day of Celebration at Poughkeepsie and Yonkers; Tuesday at Kingston, Hastings, Dobbs Ferry, Irvington and Tarrytown; Wednesday at Catskill and Nyack; Thursday at Hudson, Ossining, Haverstraw; Friday at Albany and Peekskill; and Saturday at Troy and Cold Spring. Similar ceremonies will be continued at Cohoes on Monday, Oct.11.

Appendix 2: "Looking Ahead to a Celebration in the Year 2009"
by Stephen Chalmers

This is a transcription of "Looking Ahead to a Celebration in the Year 2009: As the Clermont Seems to Us To-day So May Posterity Regard the First Crude Flying Machines of This 1909." This futuristic satire was published in *The New York Times* on September 26, 1909. The transcription is exact, so oddities of punctuation and grammar in the original have been retained. Chalmers seems to have bent the language intentionally as part of the parody.

(Editorial on "The Pioneers' Centennial" from the Universal Times, Oct. 1, A.D. 2009.)

With this year of our city, 2009, epochmaking, eramarking celebrations have come and gone—centennial exercises in honor of Henry Hudson, Robert Fulton, the Wright brothers, William Marconi, and other pioneers of last century's strides in science, industrial and otherwise.

It is the second time in our city's history that two weeks of her varied life have been given over as a mighty tribute to those men who marked the beginnings of great inventions, improvements, discoveries, and of applications which have for their result the amazing facilities for life and living afforded in this year of grace 2009.

The celebrations just ended not only mark the close of another great chapter in the history of New York; they have been an episode in the story of the universe. Since 100 years ago, when the replicas of Hudson's Half Moon and Fulton's Clermont sailed the Hudson River amid the saluting cannon of the navies of earth, times have indeed changed. The first centenary celebration was merely a local affair, gigantic though it was. The celebrations of later date have been of universal importance—the universal spirit which has characterized such functions since the reorganization of world government did away with the purely local interest.

It is curious and interesting to us at this late day to examine and compare photographs of the celebrations of 1909 with the telegravures which we print elsewhere in to-day's issue. Aside from the subject interest of these modern pictures we cannot help noticing and commenting on the change in method of production and reproduction, even in this detail of the modern arts. Yet even in the year 1909 it was no subject for incredulity that the taking and making of pictures by wireless color telephoto-gravure was about to supersede the quaint, and even then archaic, camera methods.

In the telegravures of the recent celebrations, which we publish elsewhere in this issue, we realize at a glance what has happened in this old but ever new world during the 100 years which have elapsed since the centennial's first celebration. We are at once struck by the absence of all wheeled vehicles on land and of all funneled or masted surface vessels at sea. The streets which were crowded by all sorts and conditions of more or less crude vehicles are to-day devoted to pedestrian traffic, always excepting babies' perambulators. The latter, it is interesting to recall, were at the time of which we speak the daily and particular victim of the automobile, which is now an obsolete curio, while babies and perambulators survive and have come to their own again. A nursemaid could now wheel a perambulator containing twins from the Battery to 775th Street following the middle of Broadway, and read a book undisturbed and in perfect safety—only, of course, no nursemaid would be foolish enough to essay the task on foot.

The greatest change, to return to the telegravures, is to be remarked in the sudden complete appearance of the air vessel as a landscape feature. In olden days a writer of the romantic school stated that no picture of the tropics was complete that did not contain at least a speck representing a turkey buzzard in the background. We might say that today no picture is complete that does not have an airship somewhere in the back-sky. In the celebration pictures we find the aerovessel, almost absent from the celebrations of 1909, crowding in upon the vision as cabs did around the old-fashioned theatre one hundred years ago. We find the aerovessel in its many forms—from the single-seated skimmer to the vast aerocruisers, of which the Martian type is perhaps the finest example—equivalent to the Dreadnaught of the ante-pax days. Also, we perceive along the sea coast and on the Hudson River a type of vessel which was not foreshadowed even at the time of the first centennial celebrations—the submarine and flying skimmer, is playfully sobriqued the "susky-marine." Of, course, the gradual elimination of earth and ocean surface travel made it inevitable that the submarine aerovessel should have a monopoly of the earth and the waters under the earth. It is hardly necessary to recall the case of the last of the old steel warships, the Amerigo, which foundered in 1947 with all souls after having been split by the Flying Diver (Jupiter: 2d class: 10 v. c.) as the latter shot from the ocean bed to the air leap.

The picture of last week's celebration has been vividly described in the columns of The Universal Times; also a programme of the Hudson-Fulton Celebration of 1909 was reprinted for purposes of comparison. There can be no doubt after a comparative reading that times have changed since 1909. We reproduce one portion of an article of 100 years ago. It has a quaint sound to twenty-first century ears and carries with it a suggestion of the verbiage and smallness of viewpoint which tended to mar the journalistic style of the middle American period:

> "Beginning next Saturday, Sept. 25, and continuing until Oct. 9, the State of New York will celebrate the three hundredth anniversary of the discovery of the Hudson River by Henry Hudson in 1609 and the one hundredth anniversary of the successful inauguration of steam navigation upon the same river by Robert Fulton in 1807.
>
> The first week will be New York City's City's [sic] week, although that is rather a narrow description of it, since the celebration will lap over into New Jersey and points on the lower Hudson as far as Newburg. The second week will belong to the lower upper Hudson."

"Rather a narrow description of it," indeed. But at that time world affairs were "rather narrow"—being confined to the "world." The Ramseian metal had not yet been discovered, and airship construction was still in its infancy, stumbling as yet over the problem of lighter motors. Although Prof. Blowell had received his famous message from the Grand Astronomical Axilla of Mars, Prof. Bickering had as yet refused to credit it. In fact, he died discrediting Blowell's statement that he had discovered Mars.

In the early part of the century, too, exploration had been somewhat retarded by the famous Peary-Cook controversy, in which, it will be remembered, it was conclusively shown that both men had reached the north pole, but neither of them had brought it back, the other having got it first and having refused every inducement to give it up or reveal its whereabouts. After seven years of party feeling, which rivaled the famous Dreyfus case in Paris, one Oscar Flounder of Hoboken landed on Mars in a balloon which had fourteen patches in it, and after having been called a liar on eighteen specific occasions, in nineteen different places, and always in unequivocal terms, Oscar Flounder—that is to say, Mars, was discovered. Science then forgot the north pole incident, or as it has been written in history, the "Peary-Cook Mincident."

The discovery by Prof. Ramsey of the light but durable metal which bears his name stimulated progress in aerial navigation. With the death of Mr. Flounder, following a slight accident to his famous balloon, (it went up and never came down,) the embargo—the individual copyright—on discovery was lifted. Many balunatics and aeroplanters then visited Mars and the adjacent suburbs. They found the Martians a highly refined people, who had known the use of safety matches and gum pastilles for some time.

After that, aerial navigation superseded the then paramount automobile. A fortunate circumstance in the development of aerial transportation facilities was a dispute over New York's sky-line. This dispute had been going on for some time. The question was not the necessity for an even sky-line, (this was admitted,) but whether it should be fixed at the maximum or minimum. As the maximum point would make further storeying necessary in too many cases and the minimum would require a great deal of sawing-off operations, a medium was struck, and the Mayor signed an order compelling owners of buildings to plane off, or build up, their roofs to 1,000 feet above street level. In this way a level plain was arrived at which presently became useful as a landing place for aerial liners and was highly adapted for practice speeding with skimmers.

The perfecting of the submarine, following the introduction of the airship for overland travel, produced a startling metamorphosis in general transportation. With the exception of subterranean (then called subway) transit, all traffic was by air or submarine. The improvement by Frank Reade, a boy inventor, of Jack Wright's "Flying Diver" did away with the necessity for transfer companies, and presently the world was winged, or rather, plunged—or both—into that era which had hitherto been considered in the realm of "Circling the Girdle in Eight Minutes," by the author of "Girdling the Circle In Seven," copyrighted in Great Britain by the publishers of "Squaring the Circle In Six."

As compared with the programme published yesterday of the ancient celebrations of 1909, the following programme of aerial, submarine, feathered, and aquatic sports in 2009, should suggest to the perceptive mind some of the improvements that have been effected in the last 100 years:

PROGRAMME.

The chief features of the opening day will be the rendezvous of Earthian and foreign planetary aerial vessels over the Hudson River and extending from the Baseball Grounds (roof of the Universal Times Building) to the Hackensack Terminals, (High Level.) Aerial parade of vessels of every type starting from the Narrows and circling Chicago, returning at 3 P.M., (Eastern time.)

Parade to be repeated at night, with Martian halo illuminations, Jupiterian fires, &c. and Earth, illuminated by electricity from the harnesses of Niagara Falls and Fundy tides.

Sunday will be devoted to religious observances by those accustomed to worship.

Tuesday will be devoted to the historical pageant, all nations and known planetary peoples participating, while Wednesday will be Education Day, during which the President will review, the relics of the Wright Brothers' first flying machine, the first submarine, the balloon with the fourteen patches (replica), and a sample of Prof. Koch's tuberculin.

On Thursday nothing will happen, a military parade being out of the question, but a bust of A. Carnegie, (the twentieth century Rameses) and an authentic photograph of The

Hague requiescating in pace will be exhibited to the true believers. Friday's celebrations will be held in Mars. Return tickets, (including berth on the forward aeroplanes,) $17.

The week will close with a grand procession of the planetary delegations to finish with a rendering of the "Anthem of the Starry Hosts," (Universal Keyboard.)

One of the most interesting features of the entire celebration is EXPECTED TO BE a 2,000 mile clipper aeroscat dash from New York to Chicago and return, by Dr. Scutem P. Hodges of Hoboken, and Baam Gazaab of Mars, (respectively portraying Wilbur Wright and Glenn H. Curtiss.)

We cannot refrain, in conclusion, from printing that admirably written climax of our special correspondent in describing the historic pageant as it passed the reviewing eye of President Bryan, (a great-great-great-grandson of the great-great, great Commoner:)

Slowly the birdlike monsters glided past, hung aloft the sunlight like giant Auks of the Dark Ages.

It was Man's Triumph! And below, cutting the sun-kissed waters of the Hudson with their peering gyroscopes, came the vast dark flotilla of the waters under the earth.

Beyond, upon the Palisades, darted swift flocks of skimmers, while from the level towers of Manhattan shot coveys of welcoming aeroyaks, their wings beating the thin air like the gossamer of moths and their dynamos humming like large quantities of bees confined in small bottles.

But—What is this? What draws from a million throats a sob of reminiscent grief—exquisite and refined? What relics are these that come, borne in triumph aloft the planes of yon giant cruiser? What objects are these that we venerate to-day?

A transfer ticket, mounted on a brass lion rampant; a Raines law sandwich, clutched in the teethy jaws of a Tammany tiger; an Amsterdam Avenue car, mounted on rusted rails of an ancient franchise; a Grand Street car horse, (stuffed,) loaned by the Municipal Zoo; a King, the last of his kind, loaned by the British Museum, with a ticket attached, "Do not feed or annoy his Majesty"; and—now, why do the people take off their hats?—an aeroplane, crushed and bruised and spattered with gore!

From the telephonicon three thousand feet overhead bursts a paean of music. No human musician touches the keys. The mysteries of wireless currents in ether waft the strains from far forests and waterfalls, frozen gorges, and sweltering deserts. It is the world's tribute. And now the primitive Clermont creaks and splashes through the waters, (sun-kissed,) and now comes a float, showing icebergs, bears, and gumdrops, and bearing two men and a legend, "We both done it, but he's a liar." And lastly comes a silver dollar mounted on a crystal of common salt. At that President Bryan's eyes fill and friends who are standing near see him remove his hat, and hear him murmur:

"My great-great-great-grand—" The rest is drowned in a blast of triumphal music from the overhead telephonicon. The clipper aeroscats take off on the 2,000 mile dash to Chicago and back!

Index

Note: Page numbers in *italics* refer to illustrations.

Credits

Colophon

——→◦◦←——

This book was designed and typeset by Steven Schoenfelder
in Book Antiqua, Bookman Old Style, & Futura Bold.

Print production expertise by Chris Zichello.

The paper is Goldeast Matte 128 gsm.

Prepress by Four Color Imports Digital, West Carrollton, Ohio

Printed and bound by Everbest Printing Company Ltd., China

Historic Hudson Valley

150 White Plains Road, Tarrytown, New York 10591

www.hudsonvalley.org